unearthed

BY RICH MILLER

unearthed
Eight discipleship studies to help you stand strong in hope
no matter what this world throws your way

Published by Freedom in Christ Ministries
9051 Executive Park Drive Suite 503
Knoxville, TN 37923

www.ficm.org
www.generationfreedom.org

ISBN: 9780996972536

Cover design by Mike Taylor, Taylor Graphix
taylorgraphix@knology.net
Knoxville, Tennessee

Book layout by Courtney Pierce
www.courtneypierce.net

Printed in the United States of America

contents

>> note to those using this material on your own:

You can work through the material in this book alone if you really want to. It would be a lot better, however, to try and find at least one other person with whom you can go through these studies. You will have a lot more fun and we think you will get a lot more out of it that way. As Ecclesiastes says, "Two are better than one..." (Ecclesiastes 4:9). In light of that, you'll find our approach in writing this book assumes that two or more of you are going through it together.

>> note to those in discipleship relationships:

We have set up these studies to work better if you read them and work on any assignments or short projects ahead of time. That way the participants will be familiar with the material in advance and the leader can then choose which parts to focus on during the actual meeting. Pray for those in your group each week and have fun! Don't feel that you have to cover the whole lesson in one week if you don't have time. This is designed as a eight-week study but it can easily go longer. God won't mind.

unearthed

introduction

Not too long ago I was looking out my west-facing bedroom window, admiring an amazing sunset as it transitioned from yellow to gold to orange to an almost neon-scarlet. I was marveling at its glory and the accompanying sense that our God...in addition to all His other attributes...is an Artist "sans rival."

As happens with all sunsets, the brilliant red soon turned to crimson, then to indigo and finally to a deepening gray. God's genius display of power and beauty had moved west for others to enjoy. As far as I was concerned, it was over. It was starting to get dark. But then something unexpected happened.

As I was turning back to my work, I sensed the Lord speaking to me. It was one of those cryptic messages that makes you wonder what is up. Why is He saying this to me now? Is there something imminent I need to be alerted to, or is it a word to keep on the back burner of my mind for some future season of life? Or what?

Now, if God speaking directly (not necessarily audibly but nonetheless clearly) is outside your theological comfort zone, I can understand. Admittedly, I am pretty "left-brained" and so tend to be skeptical of things that seem a bit mystical. I am keenly aware of the possibility of being deceived both by my own thoughts or the enemy's.

But Jesus did say that His sheep hear His voice (John 10:27) and so I have tried over the years to attune my ears to His Shepherd's voice and clean out any spiritual "earwax" so that I don't miss what He is saying. I'm sure I've missed a lot, but that day the message was too strong to miss.

This is what I sensed the Lord saying to my spirit:

"Don't forget the glory when the darkness comes."

I don't know if that sounds to you like something God would say, but it sounded like God to me then and it still sounds like Him to me today.

In one sense, much of Freedom in Christ Ministries is an overflow of that principle. We tell people, *no matter what accusations of guilt or shame seek to overwhelm you, remember who you are in Christ! There is no condemnation for those who are in Christ Jesus (Romans 8:1). In the face of almost debilitating fear and anxiety, stand firm in the Lord and hold up the shield of faith which promises to extinguish all the enemies' fiery arrows.* And so on.

In other words, "Don't' forget the glory when the darkness comes."

But there is another application of that principle that has prompted this writing.

As you may already know, this is the third book in the *unusual series*. Book one, *unstuck* subtitled "free from," sought to guide the reader through the disowning of wrong beliefs and the dismantling of wrong behaviors to experience the freedom for which Christ has set us free (Galatians 5:1). This is where it all starts in our discipleship and growth to maturity. You would be wise to work through that book before tackling this one, if you have not already done so.

The second book, *undaunted*, recognized that in Christ we are "free to" advance the kingdom of God. We looked at 10 arenas of ministry and examined how knowing and experiencing our identity, position, authority and freedom in Christ empowers us to serve Christ fruitfully. We are not set free to simply dance around shouting "I'm free! I'm free!" (though a certain amount of that is warranted and fun to be around!). We are also called to express our freedom by serving the Lord in the community of faith and in the hurting world around us.

Even though we are walking and growing in freedom, and have begun serving Christ...pursuing, discovering and accomplishing the good works that God has prepared for us to do (Ephesians 2:10)...we soon find that ministry is not a cakewalk. Quite the contrary. As Dr. Neil Anderson has said many times, "If we are a Christian, we are the target [of the enemy] and if we are in Christian leadership, we are the bullseye!"

We all experience suffering, every one of us. Whether we are young or old, believer or unbeliever, immature or mature, we cannot escape pain. The question is not "if" but "when" and the challenge before us is to learn to suffer well. How do we do that?

You or someone close to you might be traveling a rough road right now. Illness, injury, relational conflicts, a broken marriage, wayward children, estranged family members, financial trouble, unemployment, even the deep grief and loss of a loved one are hardships we all can face.

Believers around the world suffer from sadness, discouragement, depression, unfair criticism, deprivation, misunderstanding, gossip, slander, abuse, imprisonment, and even violence.

Suffering is universal.

At times, life is a blast and we bounce out of bed in the morning like caffeinated kangaroos. But very often, trials, tests and attacks pounce, knocking the wind out of us, flinging their massive weight upon our hearts so that we can barely breathe.

When the going gets rough, we can choose to bail as John Mark did early in his career (Acts 15:36-39) or we can be like that same John Mark who later became useful to the apostle Paul (2 Timothy 4:11) and finished strong, fulfilling his ministry despite hardship. Mark ended up writing one of the four gospels, in case you have never made the name connection before. Not too shabby!

Maybe John Mark wasn't mature enough at first to realize suffering comes with the territory of walking with and serving Christ. We don't have to make that same mistake.

In light of the inevitability of suffering in this fallen world, I have written *unearthed*, subtitled "free forever." But though I will be tackling the subject of suffering head-on, it is really a book about *hope*.

Our theme, in essence is: How does our future hope and freedom in Christ strengthen and prepare us for the suffering of today and, if we believe the Bible, the increased suffering that will precede the Second Coming of our Lord Jesus?

Our desire is that through your study of this book, "the God of all hope [will] fill you with all joy and peace in believing, so that by the power of the Holy Spirit you may abound in hope" (Romans 15:13).

This third book, like the first two, is written primarily for use in group discussion. One could certainly use it as a personal devotional for times of reflection. However, it is a lot more rewarding to grapple with these issues together with others. Plus, human nature being what it is, when we tackle topics like this alone, we are prone to skip over some sections or discussion questions. To the extent one does that, to that extent the encouragement and equipping contained in this book will be diminished.

Here are a few guidelines so that your group discussion times are the most fruitful:

- Make sure you read each study, answer any questions in the study and complete any exercises in advance of your meeting. This will greatly amplify the benefit of your time together with your group.
- When those in your group are sharing, be attentive. Don't think about what you are going to talk about; listen well. Good eye contact communicates to the one talking that you value them and what they say.
- Resist the urge to make any snide remarks or snarky comments about what someone else says, even if you know them well. There may be some in the group that are more reticent to speak and if what they say is fair game for sarcastic comments, they probably will clam up.
- When you have something you want to say, fill in enough detail to make your point or tell your story. Resist the urge to dominate and please do not give any details that are gory, erotic or otherwise unnecessary. Refrain from mentioning names of others, especially if those in your group might know the people.

If you practice these principles, everyone in the group should enjoy the studies and look forward to coming back each week.

So, what exactly will the eight studies of *unearthed* contain? Glad you asked!

A book about hope should talk about hope and that's *Study One*. We know that now "faith, hope and love all remain, but the greatest of these is love"

(1 Corinthians 13:13). I can't remember the last time I heard a sermon on the subject of "hope." Yet it is still one of the "big three," therefore we ought to know what it is and how it is meant to impact our lives. Understanding our future hope will grant us grace for today's trials.

Study Two will help you understand what in the world the "world" is. This can be a bit confusing. John 3:16 says that "For God so loved the *world*..." while later that same author warned us to not love the *world* (1 John 2:15). Huh? What does it mean to be "in the world" but not "of the world"? Understanding our place in this world and the strategies of the "god of this world" are crucial as we experience and prepare for suffering.

One of the tasks of discipleship is to help God's people learn to suffer well. That may not be very high on your priority list nor one of the gifts you'd like to find under your tree at Christmas, but since we all have suffered and will suffer again in this fallen world, it is critically important. To understand the nature of suffering, its role in our lives, and God's desired results for us are the topics of *Study Three* and *Study Four*.

Haunting the pages of Scripture as well as echoing through the hallways of history are the questions, Why, Lord?, How long, O God?, and Where are You, Lord? Sooner or later we all ask these questions and may find ourselves crying out to God in anguish and confusion. Where is God in the midst of our pain? Why does He seem so often silent? *Study Five* will examine the character of God and will seek to address these burning questions.

After these light and breezy topics (just kidding!) we will find ourselves nearing the summit of our journey. *Study Six* bursts open the treasure chest of Jesus Christ's ultimate triumph and victory over all His enemies, including pain, suffering and death. The view is amazing! It is a glimpse of the glory that we must not forget when the darkness comes.

So, what's in it for me? As good Christian people we would probably be hesitant to verbalize such a question. It sounds so...well...selfish. But the reality is that Scripture talks a lot about what is in store for the believer who perseveres to the end. What we will discuss in *Study Seven* is extremely encouraging and powerfully motivating, as we look at the rewards and glory that await us in Christ.

Finally, *Study Eight* will provide guidance to help us become the people God wants us to be in these last days. You can't jump from the couch to the starting line of the marathon and expect to do well, so I conclude this book with biblical training guidelines on how to live life in holiness and godliness, no matter what the world throws at us.

So, there you have it. I realize that this is not an easy journey we are embarking on, but it is a necessary one. Maybe you are taking a good, honest look in the spiritual mirror, realizing you are not quite in the shape you want to be (and need to be) in this fallen world. Consider this book to be a new membership at a fitness club for your soul.

Will you join me in prayer as we walk through the door to see what's inside for us?

PRAY

Dear heavenly Father, I don't remember hearing anything about suffering or endurance or even needing hope when I signed on with You and Your kingdom. It certainly wasn't in any of the "basic follow-up" material I went through early on. I do recall seeing those words as I began reading through Your Word and it was a bit unnerving at times. But I was largely able to dismiss the discomfort I felt and move on. But life won't let me ignore these realities. Stuff happens and a lot of it isn't easy. So now I'm faced with the challenge of meeting these issues head on, especially with the likelihood...if not inevitability...that life on earth is going to get rougher before we are all unearthed. So what is hope and where does it come from? Please work in me what You know I need to know, believe and practice. I want to get in better shape spiritually, maturing in my faith and becoming as much like the Lord Jesus as is possible here until You finish the work There. And if You would like to use this book in some way toward that end, then I'm in. I thank You that I am not alone in this journey and that both You and Your people are available to strengthen me as I go forward. For Your glory and Your name's renown I pray, amen.

study 1

the forgotten grace

Faith. Hope. Love. These three giants of Christian virtue fill the pages of Scripture. Though faith and love get a lot more "air time" in our churches than hope (and understandably so), if we forget *hope* in our understanding of the Christian life, it is like trying to sit on a three-legged stool with one of the legs missing. Life will be unbalanced at best, and more likely headed for a painful fall.

Because this wonderful gift is so often neglected, I have labeled hope as the *forgotten grace.*

We will begin this first study with a simple prayer. Together with those in your group, I encourage you to pray this out loud together:

PRAY

Dear heavenly Father, the apostle Paul asked that You would grant the readers of his letter to be given the Spirit of wisdom and that You would reveal Yourself so that they would all know You better. And that You would flip on the lights in their hearts so that they would know the hope to which You have called all of us (Ephesians 1:17,18). We ask that You would please do that for us as well. Amen.

An Uncertain Hope

We may be hard-pressed to recall the last time we heard a sermon preached on "hope," but we actually use the term a lot in our daily lives. Here are a few typical examples:

I sure hope that job interview goes well. There are a lot of people applying for that position.

I've heard some good things about that church. I hope we like it there.

Our team made some pretty good draft picks this year. I hope we can finally win the division.

I'm a little nervous about having all these people over. I really want us and our kids to make some friends here in the neighborhood. I hope a lot of people come and have a good time.

Often we use the word "hope" when the stakes are much higher:

The oncologist hopes that the radiation and chemo will shrink the tumor enough so that the surgery will be successful in removing all the cancer.

I really hope we are able to get pregnant. It is so hard seeing all the families with little kids at the park and all we have is our Lab.

You get the idea.

>> To get you kicked off in the right direction in your discussion group, take some time and talk about the following question. Make sure everyone gets the chance to contribute. You can learn a lot about people by listening to what they hope for. Here's the question:

What are two or three things you really hope will happen in your life, your career, your family or your future?

Use the following spaces to write down your own hopes and any of those of your fellow group members in order to remember how to pray for them this coming week. Just remember, what is spoken in the group, stays in the group!

You have probably picked up that the way we typically use the word "hope" conveys the idea of *something in the future that is a desired end*. The word "hope" can be either used as a verb (as in "I hope such and such happens...") or as a noun (as in "My biggest hope is that...").

The Bible, at times, uses *hope* in a similar way. The apostle Paul wrote to the believers in Rome: "I hope to see you in passing as I go to Spain" (Romans 15:24). And to the Christians in Corinth he wrote, "For I do not want to see you now just in passing. I hope to spend some time with you, if the Lord permits" (1 Corinthians 16:7).

There is one element of hope in all these common usages, however, that is very important to note:

All these expressions of hope have woven into them the concept of uncertainty.

In other words, we are not sure if what we hope for will happen, though we wish it would. We realize there are forces and dynamics at work that could easily derail what we are hoping for.

Depending upon how strongly we are hoping for something, a dashed hope can be anywhere from mildly disappointing to deeply disturbing...even devastating. On the other hand, a hope that actually comes about can be like a dream come true. Scripture expresses that reality:

Hope deferred makes the heart sick, but a desire fulfilled is a tree of life.
PROVERBS 13:12

A Certain Hope

Wouldn't it be awesome to be able to extract the "uncertainty" from hope and insert "certainty" instead? Well, that is exactly what happens in the primary use of the word *hope* in the Bible. Biblical hope goes way beyond human optimism, wishful thinking, our best guess or a faulty assurance based on a hopeful yet shaky foundation.

>> At this point, it will be helpful to look at a sampling of what the Bible says about hope. After each of the Scriptures below, there are blank spaces. In those spaces write what the Bible says we should put our hope in. Then write whether that object of our hope is either certain or uncertain. Then discuss in your group which of the following Scriptures means the most to you and why.

Why are you cast down, O my soul, and why are you in turmoil within me? Hope in God, for I shall again praise him, my salvation and my God.

PSALM 42:5,11; PSALM 43:5

___

___

___

You are my hiding place and my shield; I hope in your word.

PSALM 119:114

___

___

___

I wait for the Lord, my soul waits, and in his word I hope; my soul waits for the Lord more than watchmen for the morning, more than watchmen for the morning. O Israel, hope in the LORD! For with the LORD there is steadfast love, and with him is plentiful redemption. And he will redeem Israel from all his iniquities.

PSALM 1130:5-8

___

___

___

Now when Paul perceived that one [of the group to which he was speaking] were Sadducees and the other Pharisees, he cried out in the council, 'Brothers, I am a Pharisee, a son of Pharisees. It is with respect to the hope and resurrection of the dead that I am on trial.'

ACTS 23:6

For the grace of God has appeared, bringing salvation to all people, training us to renounce ungodliness and worldly passions and to live self-controlled, upright, and godly lives in the present age, waiting for our blessed hope, the appearing of the glory of our great God and Savior Jesus Christ, who gave himself for us to redeem us from all lawlessness and to purify for himself a people for his own possession who are zealous for good works.

TITUS 2:11-14

Paul, a servant of God and an apostle of Jesus Christ, for the sake of the faith of God's elect and their knowledge of the truth, which accords with godliness, in hope of eternal life, which God, who never lies, promised before the ages began...

TITUS 1:1-2

In a world where nothing is certain, not even our next breath, isn't it amazing to know that we are part of another kingdom in which hope is secure? Think about it. If you are in Christ today, your hope is sure. No matter what may happen here on earth today or tomorrow, the reservation for your one-way trip to an eternal, living, breathing, vibrant life in the new heavens and earth is confirmed. You've already checked in; your seat is waiting. No baggage needed (or wanted!).

Though the word "hope" is not specifically used in the following verses, they most definitely describe one unbelievably exciting element of our future hope: our eternally alive resurrection bodies:

For this perishable body must put on the imperishable, and this mortal body must put on immortality. When the perishable puts on the imperishable, and the mortal puts on immortality, then shall come to pass the saying that is written: "Death is swallowed up in victory." "O death, where is your victory? O death, where is your sting?" The sting of death is sin, and the power of sin is the law. But thanks be to God, who gives us the victory through our Lord Jesus Christ.

1 CORINTHIANS 15:53-57

>> These studies are designed, not only to connect us with other brothers and sisters in Christ, but to God as well. Take a few minutes in your group for different members (totally voluntary participation) to offer short prayers out loud to thank God for what His Word tells us about hope and the life that is to come. Don't worry about making lengthy or eloquent prayers. A heartfelt sentence or two in each prayer will be great.

As we saw in the Scriptures we just looked at, our hope in God's trustworthiness and His love is certain. Our hope in the truth of God's Word and its promises is certain. Our hope in the Lord Jesus Christ and His coming again is certain. Our hope in the resurrection with our new resurrection bodies is certain. Our hope in eternal life is certain...or is it?

Hope of Eternal Life

If you ask people in the church if they are certain they have eternal life now and whether they are sure they will go to heaven when they die, many will say, "I hope so." But adding the word "so" to that response reveals the individual isn't sure. Biblical faith and biblical hope indicate we are certain of the hope of eternal life. Doubt steals that certainty and puts it into the realm of an uncertain desire or simply wishful thinking.

>> In your groups you will be discussing this question, "On a scale of 1 to 10, how certain are you that you have eternal life?" In other words, do you have biblical hope (certainty) of salvation or are you just "hopeful"? Hebrews 6:11,12 says, "And we desire each one of you to show the same earnestness to have the full assurance of hope until the end, so that you may not be sluggish, but imitators of those who through faith and patience inherit the promises." Do you have the "full assurance of hope" that eternal life is yours? If so, why? If not, why not? Talk about it in your group.

Before your meeting, go ahead and write down your own response (on the 1 to 10 scale) and why you chose that level of hope:

When I was a young believer in Jesus, I struggled with the assurance of my salvation. I had come to believe that Jesus died for my sins and rose from the dead to save me, but I had doubts about where I would go when I died. At times I didn't "feel" Jesus in me; at other times I sinned and felt so guilty that I was sure the Lord had gotten disgusted with me and taken off. I asked Jesus to come into my heart so many times, I'm sure God felt pity for me; I was so confused. That is not a happy place to be. Thank the Lord for enabling me to know and believe the truth about the hope of eternal life that is ours in Christ.

If you have struggled or continue to struggle with the assurance of the hope of eternal life, you are certainly not alone. But there is hope, a true, living and lasting hope, to reassure your soul. Consider these Scriptures:

For by grace you have been saved through faith. And this is not your own doing it is the gift of God, not a result of works, so that no one may boast.

EPHESIANS 2:8-9

And this is the testimony, that God gave us eternal life, and this life is in his Son. Whoever has the Son has life; whoever does not have the Son of God does not have life. I write these things to you who believe in the name of the Son of God that you may know that you have eternal life.

1 JOHN 5:11-13

because, if you confess with your mouth that Jesus is Lord and believe in your heart that God raised him from the dead, you will be saved. For with the heart one believes and is justified, and with the mouth one confesses and is saved. For the Scripture says, "Everyone who believes in him will not be put to shame." For there is no distinction between Jew and Greek; for the same Lord is Lord of all, bestowing his riches on all who call on him. For 'everyone who calls on the name of the Lord will be saved.'

ROMANS 10:9-13

Faith, hope and love all swirl together in a supernatural movement of God to rescue us from our pitiable place of sin and death...a place out of which we could never extricate ourselves. God's love reaches us in the life, death, burial and resurrection of His Son, the Lord Jesus. God grants us the free and undeserved gift of faith in Christ that brings forgiveness. And hope bubbles forth from our faith so that we are locked onto the confident assurance of the Lord Jesus' coming again to sweep us up into the fullness of His life to experience eternity with Him.

Eternal life in Christ is both a "now" and "then" reality. We have faith now that Christ is in us and, therefore, we have eternal life already (1 John 5:11-13). But we also realize that there are elements of eternal life that are "not yet," and for that future place, future body, future freedom, future joy and future adventure, we have hope (2 Corinthians 5:1).

God wants us to know for sure. If we are in Christ, He wants us to have the unshakable, unswerving hope of eternal life...both now and in heaven when we die. If we are not in Christ, He wants us to know that, too, so we can repent and find faith, hope and love in Jesus before it is too late. It is a sobering thing to see in God's Word that those outside of Christ are described as "having no hope and without God in the world" (Ephesians 2:12). That is a very scary place to be.

>> As we will see in a moment and as we will explore during the rest of these studies, having the true hope of eternal life in Jesus will be necessary for our security, our stability, and our sanity as trials come our way. This is a really good place to pause as a group and spend some time in prayer together.

If everyone in your group indicated they were a "10" on that scale of assurance of eternal life, then great. Spend time thanking the Lord for what He has done for you and for the confident assurance and hope of eternity with Jesus.

If there are some that are unsure and still struggling with doubt, pray gently

and compassionately for them that the Lord would reveal His truth and remove all obstacles so that they can experience what the apostle Paul wrote:

For you did not receive the spirit of slavery to fall back into fear, but you have received the Spirit of adoption as sons, by whom we cry, 'Abba! Father!' The Spirit himself bears witness with our spirit that we are children of God, and if children, then heirs—heirs of God and fellow heirs with Christ, provided we suffer with him in order that we may also be glorified with him.

ROMANS 8:15-17

Today, whether you are alone or in your group, if you sense the Lord Jesus calling you into relationship with Him, and you know it's time to humble yourself and "call on the name of the Lord," I invite you to pray the following prayer out loud and from your heart:

PRAY

Dear God, it isn't good enough to just wonder or wishfully hope that I will go to heaven when I die. I need to know. I need to have the "hope of eternal life" that is not born of my own human optimism, but from Your very heart and truth. I know that I cannot save myself. All the good works in the world are not remotely sufficient to atone for my sins. My sins are like scarlet and only You can make them white as snow. The burden of my guilt and shame is overwhelming; only You can take it away. In fact, You have already done so by putting it all on Jesus as He died on the cross to pay for my sins in full. I believe that Jesus died and I also believe He didn't stay dead. He rose from the dead and is coming back one day soon. So I call on Your great Name, Jesus. Please save me and give me new life and a living hope. I thank You for making me Your child, Father, and for putting Your Holy Spirit in me. I freely choose You, Jesus, to be in charge of my life and to make me all that You created me to be, from this day forward. I declare, by the truth of Your Word and the hope of the gospel that as of this day, ________________, I now have forgiveness, new life, freedom and a living hope of eternal life through Jesus Christ. In His Name I pray, amen.

Stop and take a breath for a moment. Whether you have been in Christ and assured of the hope of eternal life for a long time, or whether this just happened to you, pause to take in the wonder of this. Heaven and our going there in Christ is not a myth, not a fable, not a legend, not a fairy tale, not wishful thinking, not even an incredible dream from which you will one day sadly wake up.

It is real. Absolutely real.

In Christ the biggest challenge of life has been resolved: *How to be freed from sin and death to enter into a relationship with God that is real, alive, joyful, fulfilling and eternal.*

Hope and Future Freedom

But the vastness of this hope goes beyond us as individuals. We are all key players in God's cosmic drama, make no mistake about it. Our lives hugely matter to God. The angels go crazy with a party when one person (like you or me!) repents and comes to Jesus (Luke 15:7,10). But the grand, sweeping, universal hope of God will one day envelop the entire creation, kicked off when God finalizes our adoption as His sons. Check this out:

For the creation waits with eager longing for the revealing of the sons of God. For the creation was subjected to futility, not willingly, but because of him who subjected it, in hope that the creation itself will be set free from its bondage to corruption and obtain the freedom of the glory of the children of God. For we know the whole creation has been groaning together in the pains of childbirth until now. And not only the creation, but we ourselves, who have the first fruits of the Spirit, groan inwardly as we wait eagerly for adoption as sons, the redemption of our bodies.

ROMANS 8:19-23

>> As our last discussion topic before we close Study One, I am going to ask you to use your imagination. As beautiful and at times, as spellbindingly majestic as nature and the whole universe is, it is screwed up. Creation itself groans, trapped in corruption. Mankind has made sure of that, unfortunately, by its sin. Take a hike in your mind through parts of the world that you know. Think about the weather, the ground and soil, the plant world, the animal kingdom, the microscopic world of nature, the cities, the countryside, the rivers, the mountains, outer space and the human race. Discuss in your group ways that our universe has been enslaved to corruption that cannot be reversed, no matter how hard we try. Here's an example to get you going: mosquitoes!

Then turn the tables. Think about some of the amazing ways things will change when Jesus makes all things new (Revelation 21:5). Talk about them in your group. Let your knowledge of God's Word and godly imaginations take you on this journey. Have fun! Example: the leopard will one day lie down with the goat (and the goat will not be *inside* the leopard! See Isaiah 11:6).

One day, all the stuff you talked about and all the myriad of other ways our world and universe are corrupted will be changed. Everything will be made new and right. Every last vestige of man's sin and its effects will be gone! Finally, the entire universe will be as it should be, as it was made to be. No more pollution. No more corruption. No more injustice. No more poverty or racism or slavery. No more headaches, backaches or heartaches. Yes, even our physical bodies will no longer groan, as we are clothed with our new resurrected bodies, free of suffering. What a day. What a hope!

None of us will be the least bit disappointed. In fact, we will all be stunned, overwhelmed with joy. It is well worth the wait. The apostle Paul finished up that news of our future freedom by writing:

For in this hope we were saved. Now hope that is seen is not hope. For who hopes for what he sees? But if we hope for what we do not see, we wait for it with patience.
ROMANS 8:24-25

I hope you now have a better grasp of how important "hope" is. It is actually indispensable and when the going gets tough for us...as we will look at in the next studies of this book, we will not be able to survive without it. The apostle Peter, writing to groups of Christians who were really going through it for their faith, said this:

Therefore, preparing your minds for action, and being sober-minded, set your hope fully on the grace that will be brought to you at the revelation of Jesus Christ.
1 PETER 1:13

What is Peter saying? When the world and all its trials come at you full force, locked and loaded, lock on to the hope that is coming one day. Earth simply cannot guarantee anything, no matter how hard we hope for it here. But this place is not all there is. There is much more to come. God promises that. One day this world will be a distant memory, if we remember it at all. Hope and the final, forever freedom that awaits you and me will enable us to endure... even triumph...no matter what this world heaves our way. No doubt about it.

I think we are ready for a definition of the biblical word *hope*.

> Hope is the confident assurance and reassurance that God will one day send the Lord Jesus back to bring all His children alive into His very presence for all eternity. In that future state, the bodies of believers will be totally remade free of sin and all creation will be recreated without corruption. And if physical death precedes His return, all who are in Christ have that same eternal home and final transformation awaiting them.

And so we will be with the Lord forever.
1 THESSALONIANS 4:17

>> Rejoice, brothers and sisters! Let's talk with God one more time before we close. I encourage you to pray the following prayer out loud together in your group:

PRAY

Dear Father, You are the God of all hope, and what You will do in the future is staggering. How can I say "Thank You!" enough for this steadfast hope? One day all my battles with sin in this world will be over and I will fully enter into the joy of salvation with You. I will be fully free from the penalty of sin, the power of sin and even the presence of sin. I have to confess, however, that right now my eyes, mind and heart are pretty set on this world. After all, this is where I live and where the people I love also live. And I know this is where You have put me so that I can grow to know and love You more deeply and minister, taking as many people with me as I can...to heaven. But, if I am honest, I think that there are some inward and outward adjustments needed regarding how I view this world and the way I live in it. I suspect that this planet and all it contains may have more of a hold on me than I think. So, as we move on in these studies, would You please open my eyes to Your kingdom and Your will for me so that I live more like the Lord Jesus here during the short time that remains until I go to You or You come for me. Thank You, Father, that I am confident that You have heard this prayer and will answer it. My hope is in You. Amen.

study 2

earthed

When you first saw the title of this book, *unearthed*, maybe you thought it was a little unusual. That was intentional. Usually when we think of something being "unearthed," we think of something buried that is brought back to the surface either literally or figuratively. Relics from the past, time capsules, even old bones are unearthed. So are memories and pieces of evidence in a cold criminal case.

But this is not a book on archaeology, history, paleontology, psychotherapy or even forensic science. It is a book about living life well on the surface of planet Earth, both now and in the days to come. You'll see more of why I entitled this book *unearthed* in the pages ahead.

>> To get you warmed up to this second study that I am calling "Earthed," I'd like you to talk about the concept of "home" for a few minutes. Discuss together where you grew up (even if that means multiple locales). If you feel comfortable, talk about whether the place(s) you called home as a kid or teen are filled with good or not-so-good memories. What place do you consider to be your home now? Why? What are the qualities that make a place not just a residence, but a home? This is another opportunity to get to know one another in your group and, once again, gain some valuable insight for praying for each other.

Use the spaces on the next page to jot down any notes from the discussion that will help you remember things about your fellow discussion group members and pray for them this coming week:

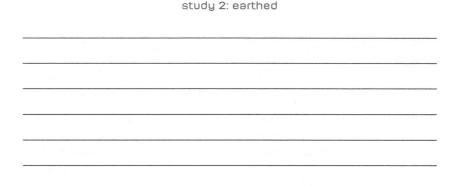

When traveling, I often get asked where I'm from. I live in western North Carolina, near Asheville, which often elicits ooh's and aah's from people familiar with this beautiful part of the country. If I were to be totally truthful, though, I should probably respond, "Well, I live near Asheville, North Carolina, but that is not my home." That might raise some eyebrows, and also could lead to some interesting discussions!

You may have already figured out where I'm going with this. To paint the full picture, however, let's take a step back and look for a moment at this world in which we live...this planet we typically call "home."

The Bible is clear on several matters of foundational importance:

The World Defined

- First, God is the Creator of the world we see around us.

  "And the angel whom I saw standing on the sea and on the land raised his right hand to heaven and swore by him who lives forever and ever, who created heaven and what's in it, the earth and what is in it, and the sea and what is in it..." (Revelation 10:6)

- Second, by virtue of His being Creator, God is the Lord of this world. In other words, He is in charge.

  "At the end of the days I, Nebuchadnezzar, lifted up my eyes to heaven, and my reason returned to me, and I blessed the Most High, and praised and honored him who lives forever, 'for his dominion is an everlasting dominion, and his kingdom endures from generation to generation; all the inhabitants of the earth are accounted as nothing, and he does according to his will among the host of heaven and among the inhabitants of the earth; and none can stay his hand or say to him, 'What have you done?'"" (Daniel 4:34,35)

In response to God, the Lord of all, the 24 elders in heaven fall down before the Father, worshiping Him and casting their crowns before Him saying, 'Worthy are you, our Lord and God, to receive glory and honor and power, for you created all things, and by your will they existed and were created" (Revelation 4:10,11).

>> Remember what I said in the first study about this being a group time to connect with God (as well as with one another)? Toward that end, take a few minutes and invite those in the group to worship our God and Lord out loud for who He is.

Worship should engage every part of us—including our emotions and bodies. Let the Spirit lead you but know it's okay to be enthusiastic! Scripture says:

Hallelujah! Praise God in his holy house of worship, praise him under the open skies; praise him for his acts of power, praise him for his magnificent greatness; praise with a blast on the trumpet, praise by strumming soft strings; praise him with castanets and dance, praise him with banjo and flute, praise him with cymbals and a big bass drum, praise him with fiddles and mandolin. Let every living, breathing creature praise God! Hallelujah!

PSALM 150 (MSG)

>> Join your voices with the 24 elders in heaven. Let your hearts be reminded and your spirits refreshed in remembering God and honoring Him as the Lord of all.

Okay, time to get back down to earth. When the Bible talks about the "world," it can refer to all of creation (and particularly planet Earth). God is the Creator and Lord of that world, our world. We just saw and acknowledged that truth together.

The term "world" in the Bible can also refer to the population of people on the earth. That is what is meant in John 3:16: *"For God so loved the world, that He gave his only Son, that whoever believes in him should not perish but have eternal life."* God loves people. He loves the whole human race and does not want anyone to perish but for all to repent and turn to Him (2 Peter 3:9).

There is another way in which the Bible uses the term "world," and this is the usage that we will primarily focus upon in this study.

>> Go ahead and read the following Bible verses out loud in your group. Then follow the prompts below for your group that come after those Scriptures.

If the world hates you, know that it has hated me before it hated you. If you were of the world, the world would love you as its own; but because you are not of the world, but I chose you out of the world, therefore the world hates you.
JESUS'S WORDS IN JOHN 15:18,19

If you love me, you will keep my commandments. And I will ask the Father, and he will give you another Helper, to be with you forever, even the Spirit of truth, whom the world cannot receive, because it neither sees him nor knows him. You know him, for he dwells with you and will be in you.
JESUS'S WORDS IN JOHN 14:15-17

And the great dragon was thrown down, that ancient serpent, who is called the devil and Satan, the deceiver of the whole world—he was thrown down to the earth, and his angels were thrown down with him.
REVELATION 12:9

We know that everyone who has been born of God does not keep on sinning, but he who was born of God protects him, and the evil one does not touch him. We know that we are from God, and the whole world lies in the power of the evil one.
1 JOHN 5:18-19

>> Taking the revelations from God in these four Scripture passages, discuss together what the Bible is talking about in this usage of the term "world." Then, consolidate what you have gleaned from these verses and, together, come up with a consensus definition of the "world" as you see it described in the verses above. Do your best in about 7-10 minutes of discussion time to nail the essence of what the word "world" means here.

Use the following spaces to take notes from your group discussion:

>> Go ahead and write your group's consensus definition in the following space:

____

____

____

____

____

You may have heard that, as Christians, we have three enemies: the world, the flesh and the devil. My observation of folks in the Church is that we tend to be pretty aware of the influence of our own flesh (our human, sinful propensity to live independently from and disobediently toward God). Overcoming the flesh and its tendencies is another matter, but ignorance of this ungodly dynamic at work inside us is rare.

In addition, depending upon the particular church, disciples of Jesus can have anywhere from a nominal to an extensive awareness of the devil and his strategies. We ought not to be ignorant of the devil's schemes (2 Corinthians 2:11), but unfortunately, many are.

Both the "flesh" and the devil are topics discussed thoroughly in the book *unstuck*.

My main concern in this study is to shine light on the reality and operation of the world system. This system is under the control of the evil one and stands in opposition to Jesus. Sadly, many Christians are largely blind to the impact of the world system on their lives, and in fact, tolerate much of it.

For our purposes, I will describe this usage of the "world" as follows:

> The world involves... aspects of every culture, governed by the evil one, that have been infiltrated by and even saturated with the belief and practice of ignoring, marginalizing, demeaning or antagonistically opposing God and His Word; this includes all the counterfeit gods (false sources of "life" and "joy") as well as all the stuff that distracts and detours people from knowing or fully following Christ.

>> Discuss in your group what you think of that definition. Is it clear? Is there anything that you came up with that is not contained in this suggested definition of "the world"? If so, what is it? Then, see if each group member can come up with at least one example of the world that fits your description and mine. Try and make the examples as relevant to your daily lives as possible. Example: new car ads on TV that try and convince you that owning one of their vehicles will make you happy, important, satisfied, admired and free.

You can take notes in the spaces following, writing down any good examples of "the world" and especially things you hadn't thought of before:

Our Place in This World

In summary, we all live in the world (created, overseen and governed by God). Within God's world, there operates another world, a world system, that is governed by the devil. The Church (the body of true born again believers in Jesus) is living in the larger God-world, but it has been taken out of the smaller world system that the evil one controls. 1 John 5:4,5 makes it clear that we have already overcome this evil world system by our faith in Jesus:

For everyone who has been born of God overcomes the world. And this is the victory that has overcome the world – our faith. Who is it that overcomes the world except the one who believes that Jesus is the Son of God?

1 JOHN 5:4-5

Jesus described our being "in the world" (i.e. living on planet Earth) but not "of the world" (i.e. not buying into the values of the godless world system). So, in one sense, we are "out of this world" (Jesus' words in John 15:19), though we are not out of our minds (2 Timothy 1:7 NKJV), as some people might believe.

Confused? Let's try and clarify things a bit.

>> First, we need to address the question, "How is someone who lives on planet Earth and has been called out of the ungodly world system to "be in the world but not of it" supposed to identify himself or herself? Look at the following Scriptures and circle any words or phrases that give a clue as to the answer to that question.

All this is from God, who through Christ reconciled us to himself and gave us the ministry of reconciliation; that is, in Christ God was reconciling the world to himself, not counting their trespasses against them, and entrusting to us the message of reconciliation. Therefore, we are ambassadors for Christ, God making his appeal through us. We implore you on behalf of Christ, be reconciled to God.
2 CORINTHIANS 5:18-20

But our citizenship is in heaven, and from it we await a Savior, the Lord Jesus Christ, who will transform our lowly body to be like his glorious body, by the power that enables him even to subject all things to himself.
PHILIPPIANS 3:20-21

Dear friends, I warn you as 'temporary residents and foreigners' to keep away from worldly desires that wage war against your very souls.
1 PETER 2:11 NLT

>> Write in the following spaces any words or phrases you circled from God's Word that describe who we are (in Christ) in relation to the world:

____

____

____

____

>> There are a variety of ways we can view ourselves in relation to this world. We can see ourselves as citizens; tourists; prisoners; ministers; residents; visitors; ambassadors; foreigners; friends; etc. Discuss in your groups what words you listed in the blanks above that indicate who we are in God's eyes. Then talk about how you actually view yourselves. Be honest! If there is a discrepancy between how you view your place in this world versus who God says you are in Christ, seek to unearth in discussion together some of the reasons why that might be the case.

I would tend to use the following words to describe or identify myself: Christian or child of God, man, husband, father, American, minister, author, middle-aged person (I'm in denial), sports fan, and a few other terms depending on my particular mood at the moment. Your list will vary depending on your gender, age, marital status, vocation and other aspects of your life you deem important.

Whether we believe it or not, who God says we are at the center of our being is our primary and most important identity. You could call it our "core identity." In Christ, we are no longer children of the devil (John 8:44). We are children of God and knowing this truth and all that it entails is crucial to our daily victory in this world.

This critical topic was also addressed in *unstuck*.

I don't know about you, but I need continual reminders that I am an ambassador, a minister of reconciliation, a citizen of heaven, a foreigner, and a temporary resident of this world.

To forget these (and other) parts of our "spiritual résumé" in Christ will have a serious dulling and darkening effect on our lives in this world, as we are about to see. Just as, in Christ, we are dead to sin but alive to God (Romans 6:1-7), so in Christ we have overcome the world (1 John 5:4,5). But can sin still prevail and control us as followers of Christ? Certainly. In the same way, the world system also can subtly infiltrate our beliefs and behaviors if we are not careful.

Our Enemy: The World

We who have already overcome the world by our faith in Jesus can subtly find ourselves being overcome by the world instead.

What we have looked at so far in Study Two has been critical for laying the foundation. We are now moving into the heart of this second study, and it would be very appropriate to take a moment to pray.

>> In your group, together, pray the following prayer out loud:

PRAY

Dear heavenly Father, I am aware of the physical world around me through my five senses. But You say in Your Word that there is another world operating around me that is hostile to You. I confess that many times I am unaware of its presence and its attempts to pull me back in though You have already rescued me from it. Open my eyes, Lord! Help me to see honestly how this enemy both of my soul and Your kingdom is influencing me. Grant me repentance, dear Lord, for the ways I have been deceived and seduced by it. This will probably mean some adjustments to my life. Give me the conviction and courage to do all that is needed to be liberated to live as a free citizen of heaven, serving as Your ambassador here until You come. Amen.

Disciples of Jesus have struggled with being taken in by the world system ever since the Church was born and the New Testament was written. This is nothing new. In fact, the devil has used the same strategies all throughout history to try and trip up God's people. He did so successfully with Eve (see Genesis 3) but unsuccessfully with Jesus (see Matthew 4).

The only things that have changed over the years are the things the god of this world system has utilized for his purposes. Stuff changes, and Satan is always very "state-of-the-art." There is always something new coming out to attract our attention (and money!). The basic strategies, however, have not changed. 1 John 2:15-17 (NASB) spells out what these three strategies are:

Do not love the world nor the things in the world. If anyone loves the world, the love of the Father is not in him. For all that is in the world, the lust of the flesh and the lust of the eyes and the boastful pride of life, is not from the Father, but is from the world. The world is passing away, and also its lusts, but the one who does the will of God lives forever.

1 JOHN 2:15-17

A lust is a strong desire that overtakes us and becomes the reigning desire of our heart (see James 1:13-15).

The lust of the flesh, then, would be any strong and controlling appetite for ease, comfort or pleasure that is outside God's perfect will for us.

The lust of the eyes involves being captivated and captured by the desire for things we see. We want what we want when we want it, and we feel entitled to it.

The boastful pride of life is all that we accomplish and broadcast to others in an attempt to get people to notice us, admire us, defer to us, want to listen to us and be around us. It is our sinful drive for popularity, fame, acclaim, control and power over others. At some sick level, our flesh wants people to worship us.

There are clues from our emotions and behavior that can indicate one or more of these three strategies of the world is working on us and in us. They include:

- Restlessness
- Drivenness
- Discontent
- Anxiety
- Insecurity
- Impure thoughts and motives
- Greed
- Control and manipulation
- Envy and jealousy
- Inability to listen
- Tendency to compare and be hyper-competitive
- Domination of conversations
- Power struggles

>> Before we dive into an analysis of what "loving the world" means and how it shows up in our lives, take a few minutes, first by yourself and then in your group to consider the following questions (based on 1 John 2:15-17).

How does a simple interest in or curiosity about something in the world become an unhealthy and unholy lust of the flesh or of the eyes? What are a couple examples of the boastful pride of life that you see operative in your life? How does the love of things crowd out our love for God the Father?

Before your meeting, write down in the spaces below your answers to the questions above. That will help you think through what this Scripture is teaching and prepare you well for the upcoming discussion:

1 John 2:15-17 makes it clear that life on this earth is a battle over who and what we will love above all else. Jesus said that the two greatest commandments are:

> ***You shall love the Lord your God with all your heart and with all your soul and with all your mind. This is the great and first commandment. And a second is like it: You shall love your neighbor as yourself. On these two commandments depend all the Law and the Prophets.***
>
> MATTHEW 22:37-39

Though we are told that our greatest priorities in life are to love God and people, we can easily end up loving this world and what is in it instead. With obvious grief in his heart, the apostle Paul wrote to Timothy about one of the men traveling with him:

> ***Do your best to come to me soon. For Demas, in love with this present world, has deserted me and gone to Thessalonica."***
>
> 2 TIMOTHY 4:9-10

We are not immune to the spiritual disease that captured Demas' heart. I call this spiritual malady of loving this present world being "Earthed," and it means we have allowed this evil world system and its values to bury its claws deeply into our hearts. We need to be *unearthed.*

> To understand what loving the world looks like, we need to have a basic understanding of the nature of love itself.

Love involves an attachment to someone or something that results in a commitment to serve that one or thing sacrificially. "Love" without attachment is just duty. Attachment without sacrificing self is ultimately self-serving, and not love at all.

When we are attached to something (or someone), we think about it a lot; we spend time with it as much as we can; we miss it when it is not around; we choose it above other things; and we adjust our schedule to it. We might even be willing to die for it, though more commonly we just end up living for it. The danger is that we can end up sacrificing an important object of love for one that is of far less importance.

Jesus warned of this danger:

No one can serve two masters, for either he will hate the one and love the other, or he will be devoted to the one and despise the other. You cannot serve God and money.

MATTHEW 6:24

In our affluent Western society, many have tried to do just that—serve both God and money. But it doesn't work. It can't work. Money can be a useful servant but it is a cruel master.

Ecclesiastes 5:10 (NIV) says:"Whoever loves money never has enough; whoever loves wealth is never satisfied with their income."

Those words were written by King Solomon, the richest man of his day. He knew what he was talking about. Why would we think we know better?

Though we are allowed to use money as a tool, we are never given permission to love it. If we truly love God, money will be our servant as we serve Christ, and we find God loving us powerfully and continually in return. But if we love money, we will find it incapable of loving us back. Money and the objects it can buy are soulless, lifeless, hollow and empty things, only capable of giving us temporary pleasure. But there is no warranty with "stuff" that it will bring joy 12 months or even 12 days from now, only the guarantee of a restless yearning for more.

Becoming Unearthed

>> The following exercise ideally should be fully completed prior to the group meeting. If needed, a few minutes can be taken during the meeting to allow for members to finish it. This is a very important exercise and should neither be bypassed nor rushed through.

As you will see below, I have created a continuum of your attachments to things of the world. The first column refers to a healthy level in which that

area is not a threat to your love for God. As you proceed to the right, the levels of attachment increase.

Make a mark along that line as to where you believe you stand with each of these areas. Be honest. Don't just assume you are living at a "healthy" level in each area. Let the Holy Spirit enable you to see things the way He does. Following that exercise, there will be a prayer of repentance that will help you face and then turn your heart away from the things the Lord has pointed out are rivals to your highest love for Him.

Attachment Analysis of Rivals to God

	Healthy	Growing Interest	Frequent Focus	Constant Habit	Obsession
Accumulating Wealth					
Home Upgrades					
New Clothes					
Tech Gadgets					
Social Media					
Cell Phone					
Fitness					
Politics					
Food					
Shopping					
Sports					

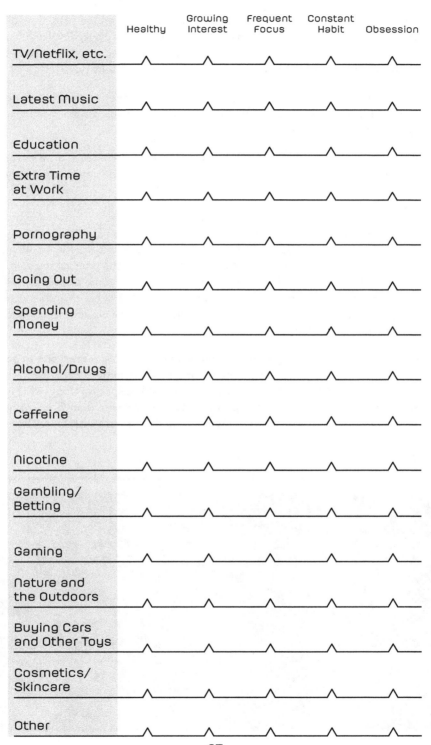

	Healthy	Growing Interest	Frequent Focus	Constant Habit	Obsession
TV/Netflix, etc.					
Latest Music					
Education					
Extra Time at Work					
Pornography					
Going Out					
Spending Money					
Alcohol/Drugs					
Caffeine					
Nicotine					
Gambling/ Betting					
Gaming					
Nature and the Outdoors					
Buying Cars and Other Toys					
Cosmetics/ Skincare					
Other					

Ultimately, we can have only one "first love." If we love God first, then all the love we need for our fellow man will be an outflow and overflow from our primary attachment to Him. And we will find our attraction and attachment to this world and the things of the world decreasing in intensity.

If we love something or someone else more than God, then to that degree we lose our love for God and man. As a friend of mine has said, "Sin starts to looks good when God doesn't."

Again, this is a battle for love, a battle for our hearts. Whatever or whoever captivates your heart will capture your heart. If that isn't Jesus, it will only lead to false hope.

Perhaps the Lord has shown you that some things are out of whack in your heart. You know you need to and want to change direction and return to your first love, making God your number one heart attachment once again. If so, here is a prayer to begin that process. Like the father in the prodigal son story (Luke 15:11-32), God the Father waits eagerly for you to come to your senses and come back home. He will embrace you, put the robe of honor and sandals of sonship on you, place the ring of His authority back on your finger and commence the celebration!

>> Take some time during your group meeting now to allow everyone to go off by themselves. Encourage group members to look honestly at their lives and to use the following prayer to confess to God the specific things of this world that have become more important and central to life than God. Make sure you allow sufficient time for members to do business with God. There is no need to rush.

PRAY

Dear heavenly Father, I remember when Jesus told the parable of the four soils, that there was one soil in which thorns sprang up and choked out the Word so that there was no fruit. Those thorns represented "the cares of the world, the deceitfulness of riches and the desires for other things" (Mark 4:18,19). That's what we are talking about in this study, isn't it? I have asked You to open my eyes and shine the light on my heart so I might clearly see the rivals that have been raised up to try and steal my love for You. This is no small matter, for You have said that we shall have no other gods before You (Exodus 20:3). I confess that I have allowed (name the things the Lord has shown you from the Attachment Analysis) to become more important to me than You. I repent of this sin and turn away from it, asking You to help me to radically deal with these thorns. Despite how much I have enjoyed them in the past, thorns are harmful and, in this spiritual sense, are evil. Thank You for Your forgiveness. I now ask You to fill me with the Holy Spirit so that I will not fulfill the lust of the flesh, the lust of the eyes or the boastful pride of life. Those things are not from You but are from the world. And this world is fast becoming obsolete, along with all its lusts, but I know that if I do Your will, I will live forever. Amen.

You have taken an important first step in becoming *unearthed*. There are more steps to come. Don't be surprised if people in your world don't understand any radical steps you have to take in order to get freed up from the sticky web of this world system. Ask the Lord to show you what He wants you to do.

As you perhaps see more clearly now, it is easy to become "conformed to this world" when you desperately need to be "transformed by the renewing of your mind" (Romans 12:2).

This world in which we now live is not our real home. Heaven is. But while we are here, we have the incredible privilege and opportunity to serve as agents of heaven, ambassadors for Christ, holy representatives of another kingdom to the world of people God loves. (See *undaunted* for practical help in how to do this.) While we are about our Father's business here on the earth, we need to keep in mind that this world system, run by the evil one, is never our friend (James 4:4).

God is committed to making sure you and I are increasingly *unearthed*, and He has another strategy to ensure that happens. It is His powerful tool of suffering, and is the subject of our next study.

study 3

God's megaphone

C.S. Lewis wrote, "God whispers to us in our pleasures, speaks in our conscience, but shouts in our pain. It is His megaphone to rouse a deaf world."[1]

Lewis, though well-known for writing *The Chronicles of Narnia* and many books on defending the Christian faith, was no stranger to suffering. His book, *A Grief Observed*, written while mourning the loss of his beloved wife, Joy Gresham, is almost too much for the reader to bear. His depictions of the raw agony and loss he was experiencing are brutally graphic.

Elisabeth Elliot, who battled cancer and the death of two husbands (one of whom was martyred as a missionary to the Huaorani people in a remote part of Ecuador) said this regarding suffering:

> "I'm convinced that there are a good many things in this life that we really can't do anything about, but that God wants us to do something with."[2]

It is our belief that both Elisabeth Elliot and C.S. Lewis are right. Everyone suffers. It comes with the territory here on our fallen planet. It is a wake-up call. The question is not whether you and I will suffer but how well we handle it. Though suffering is about experiencing pain and loss, that is not all it is. It is also about a difficult, sometimes perplexing, often desperately lonely journey to discover God in its midst.

How do we hold on to hope in the midst of pain and suffering?

>> As you begin this third study, what you encounter on these pages may be personal to you. You may be going through some very difficult tests right now or perhaps someone you know and love is in that place. In your group, I'd like to give opportunity for those currently experiencing pain the freedom to talk about their suffering. It doesn't have to be a huge, life threatening situation (though it can be).

This should not be in any way a competition as to who should be pitied the most. That's not what this is all about. Pain is pain and suffering is suffering and it is hard for all of us to go through it. Once the sharing is complete, take some time to pray for one another for God's comfort and mercy in the midst of pain. Pray also that these studies would provide meaningful encouragement. Please avoid using this time to give counsel or advice to those who are suffering.

Use the spaces following to jot down any quick notes about the struggles of your fellow group members. This is for the purpose of prayer only. Do not share these with anyone outside the group unless the group member specifically mentions it is okay to do so. Be a person who can be totally trusted!

____

____

____

____

____

____

____

>> After your time of praying for one another is finished, I encourage you to pray the following prayer out loud together:

PRAY

Dear heavenly Father, to be perfectly honest, I don't like to suffer, but it is especially difficult to endure when the pain seems pointless. If I can figure out some reason as to why I or someone else is going through a rough time, I'm more okay with that. But when I see reports of things like the latest school shooting or a young child dying of cancer, I really struggle with the pain that those who are grieving have to go through. And the world is full of examples like that. It just doesn't seem fair.

Sometimes I even feel a twinge of guilt for having escaped that kind of pain, at least so far. I know You understand all this and I also know that if there is anyone in the universe that can make sense of these things, it is You. Please help me to sort this out and come to a place of some kind of settled-ness until I am fully unearthed and you can explain it all to me in heaven, if You so choose. Thank You that You are a good God. Amen.

Some level of self-disclosure here is in order. I am by no means some kind of expert on suffering. I can't imagine anyone wanting that role anyway. Sure, I've suffered like everyone else. But I am just an author. The only credential I bring to this table is that I believe the Lord has called me to write this. Trust me, I undertake this task reluctantly and with fear and trepidation. The two things I dread most are a) misrepresenting God and His Word and b) coming across as insensitive to those who are suffering in ways I can only have nightmares about. Fortunately, I have been able to listen to some who have suffered deeply and come through to the other side. My prayer is that some of what these godly people have taught me might be communicated on these pages.

Mankind Messes Things Up

Let's begin our study by looking at how suffering came about in the first place.

You might remember that in God's original creation in the Garden of Eden, everything was just right. God called it "very good." A tropical nudist colony for two with perfect weather, totally cool animals that were all friendly, the best food ever grown right at your fingertips... It was like Bali, Costa Rica, Maui and the Caribbean all put together, but with nothing bad at all. Who can beat that? No pollution or trash, sickness, pain, conflict, injury, sadness, loss, or death. Nothing remotely nasty; it was all good. You can read about it in Genesis 2. That was God's work.

Then along came a snake. Not a creepy, slithery, scary thing but likely an attractive, intelligent, upright, talking serpent, though possessed by Satan and therefore evil to the core. Make no mistake. How the devil managed to crash this party, I don't know, but he was there. Poo-pooing the Word of God which warned Adam that in the day he ate from the tree of the knowledge of good and evil he would die, the devil tricked Eve into eating the forbidden fruit. Adam listened to his wife and ate also, and all hell broke loose.

Suffering was born. That was man's work.

>> Before your meeting, on your own, take a few minutes and read Genesis 3:1-19. Then fill in the blanks below with how God's perfect world was immediately corrupted into the sin-wrecked world we live in now. When you come to your meeting, have someone read that same passage of Genesis 3:1-19 out loud. Then talk about your answers (written below) in your group.

No shame and complete innocence became ____________________

Being comfortable in their own skin became ____________________

Enjoying God and His presence became ____________________

Perfect harmony between Adam and Eve became ____________________

A safe and easy process of bearing children became ____________________

Meaningful, productive work in the Garden became ____________________

Life forever in the Garden of Eden became ____________________

To borrow an image from mythology, when man sinned, Pandora's Box was flung wide open. Like a filthy, toxic nuclear explosion of astronomical portions, the effects of sin spread to and permeated every corner of creation. The perfect DNA of the universe and all that was in it became fatally flawed in that one instant. From the smallest cell of man and woman to the farthest star in the most distant galaxy, sin left no victim unscathed by corruption.

Where before man and woman had been naked and unashamed, they instantly became self-conscious, anxious, insecure and obsessed with covering up. How did they even know what parts of their bodies to cover? Whereas before they had not even been aware of their nakedness, they immediately felt vulnerable, unprotected and uncovered. Shame and guilt washed over humanity like a sick tsunami.

A close, easy, beautiful relationship with God was suddenly gone. They trembled and hid in a grove of trees. They must have lost their minds, actually thinking they could hide from the all-knowing, all-seeing God of the universe...? Fear and madness were born, as was spiritual death (separation from God ultimately resulting in physical death).

The honeymoon was over. The blame game started between Adam and Eve and relationships have been strained by accusations, self-protection, blaming and shaming ever since. The seeds of marital conflict and divorce were sown. The resultant wounding in the hearts of countless men and women, boys and girls throughout history is incalculable.

Pain was created. Decreed initially for childbirth, it spread to all of life on this fallen planet, including the work of our hands. Every dead-end job, every tyrannical employer, every unfair labor practice, every sweat shop and blight of slavery can be traced back to here.

The destruction of life and the decay and decomposition of human (and all other) matter began. Think about this reality: All doctors, medicines, medical clinics, hospitals, funerals, and cemeteries have resulted from one act of disobedience by our first parents. Not to mention the whole need for law enforcement, the criminal justice system and many other occupations.

Paradise was lost with no way man could ever find his way back again.

Sin is by far the most destructive force for evil in the entire history of the world. It is the deadliest weapon of mass destruction ever created.

This was all mankind's fault, but so often God Himself gets blamed for suffering. That is not fair. God's Word says:

The foolishness of man ruins his way, and his heart rages against the LORD.
PROVERBS 19:3 NASB

But God, in His grace, opened the door of hope a crack even on such a dark and deadly day (Genesis 3:15). We shall see that hope in much fuller glory later in this book.

God Uses Man's Mess

No question about it. All the temporary suffering mankind has endured throughout the centuries has been terrible. No one knows that better than God. He has seen it all. But the prospect of eternal suffering makes everything else pale by comparison. God does not want anyone to perish and so, as C.S. Lewis, noted, God needed a megaphone to wake up a deaf and slumbering human race.

God has chosen to allow pain as one of His tools to grab our attention before it is too late.

Making the valid assumption, I trust, that most readers of this book are already followers of Jesus, it is probably of great interest to you to know how God uses suffering for His glory and our good as believers. The Church needs God's megaphone as well. I love the title of Elisabeth Elliot's book: *Suffering is Never for Nothing*.

>> Before addressing this very relevant topic, take some time in your group to talk about the times (either before you knew Christ or since you received Him as Savior and Lord) when you went through a painful but life-changing time. It would be helpful for you to think about this in advance of your meeting so you come to the group being prepared to talk about something specific in your own journey. Then in your group meeting, talk about how that time of struggle/suffering changed you.

Author Neil Anderson provides a great visual. He says that going through trials is like God pulling you through a knothole. It will not be easy and in fact will certainly be painful. But when you eventually pop out the other side, you will be in a lot different shape than when you went in. How have God's knotholes changed you? How have you seen that suffering indeed is "never for nothing" in your life? This can be a really meaningful group discussion time.

One of the things that jumps out when you look at Scripture is that God is big enough to use the nastiest things of life for His good purposes. One of the best short stories in all of the world's literature is the saga of how Joseph's brothers treated him like dirt, but God intervened and mined precious gold out of that muck.

If you haven't read Genesis 37-50 in a while, it's well worth the read. Joseph's conclusion of the matter is important for us to remember. His brothers were terrified that Joseph, whom God raised up to be second in command over all Egypt, would take revenge on them, once their father, Jacob, died. He reassured his brothers that he meant them no harm, saying:

> ***Do not fear, for am I in the place of God? As for you, you meant evil against me, but God meant it for good, to bring about that many people should be kept alive, as they are today.***
>
> GENESIS 50:19-20

That is an Old Testament prologue to some very helpful New Testament Scriptures.

>> Read the Scriptures below out loud in your group and discuss your answers to the questions that follow. Honestly talk about whether you are able to believe what the Bible is saying in these verses or whether your experience and feelings are sending you a different message. There are blank spaces below in which you can write down your answers to those questions in advance. Individual preparation for group discussion always makes the discussion richer.

Therefore, since we have been justified by faith, we have peace with God through our Lord Jesus Christ. Through him, we have also obtained access by faith into this grace in which we stand, and we rejoice in hope of the glory of God. Not only that, but we rejoice in our sufferings, knowing that suffering produces endurance, and endurance produces character, and character produces hope, and hope does not put us to shame, because God's love has been poured into our hearts through the Holy Spirit who has been given to us.

ROMANS 5:1-5

Count it all joy, my brothers, when you meet trials of various kinds, for you know that the testing of your faith produces steadfastness. And let steadfastness have its full effect, that you may be perfect and complete, lacking in nothing.

JAMES 1:2-4

And we know that for those who love God all things work together for good, for those who are called according to his purpose. For those whom he foreknew he also predestined to be conformed to the image of his Son, in order that he might be the firstborn among many brothers.

ROMANS 8:28-29

>> What is the primary emotion God wants us to experience when going through trials and suffering? How is that even possible? What does God's Word say He is doing in us "behind the scenes" during the times we find our faith is tested that would give us cause to rejoice? According to these Scriptures, are all things "good"? What does the Bible say actually is good? What is God's supreme plan for His children?

Here is some space to write down your thoughts in advance. You may also want to jot down notes from what others in your group share. They likely will have insights that you hadn't thought of:

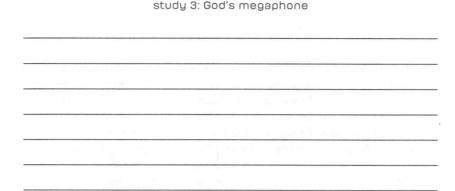

Obviously, what the apostles Paul and James are saying here are not easy words. If I were to describe my typical reaction to trials, especially as a young Christian, I would say, "Brothers, when things get rough, don't do as I do, which is to complain. I tend to fuss and fume and even utter a mild curse under my breath and bemoan how unfair life is."

In those days, when I read some Scriptures (like those above) I shook my head and wondered how much more unrealistic the Bible could get.

By the grace of God, I'm changing my view of trials. It doesn't happen all at once for any of us, but little by little we can move toward the goal of what those two apostles were counseling us to do: considering trials all joy instead of all misery. It turns out those two men weren't being *unrealistic* at all; they were actually being *therapeutic*. Rejoicing and giving thanks and praying (see 1 Thessalonians 5:16-18) actually release good hormones in the brain that generate joy and help us make it through tough times. God thought of that!

A Magnet to Suffering

When it comes to people talking about what they are going through, I like to consider the source. Let's consider the source of two of these Scriptures...the apostle Paul. Aside from his writing being inspired by the Holy Spirit (which brings totally sufficient credence to what he wrote) does Paul have any experiential credentials to stand on? Actually yes. Here are his words, defending his apostleship against critics who had the gall to take him on:

Are they servants of Christ? I am a better one—I am talking like a madman—with far greater labors, far more imprisonments, with countless beatings, and often near death. Five times I received at the hands of the Jews the forty lashes less one. Three times I was beaten with rods. Once I was stoned. Three times I was shipwrecked; a night and a day I was adrift at sea; on frequent journeys, in danger from rivers, danger from robbers, danger from my own people, danger from the Gentiles, danger in the city, danger in the wilderness, danger at sea, danger from false brothers; in toil and hardship, through many a sleepless night, in hunger and thirst, often without food, in cold and exposure.
2 CORINTHIANS 11:23-27

When it comes to suffering as a Christian, the apostle Paul leaves most of us in the dust. It was like he was a magnet for suffering.

And this isn't even all of it. Paul was responsible for many churches and many followers of Jesus and he had to go through the agony of watching them struggle and suffer as well. It is often harder to endure the suffering of a loved one than it is to endure one's own. Paul did both.

We can accept Paul's counsel in how to deal with trials and suffering as "the truth, the whole truth and nothing but the truth" because a) he was inspired by the Holy Spirit, b) he suffered tons more than just about any of us and c) he practiced what he preached...he had learned to rejoice in all of it.

By the way, a comment about one of Paul's verses is in order. Romans 8:28 does not say that everything is good. The expression that people smugly spout off in the midst of pain, "It's all good!," is simply not true. For His children, God is able to turn the worst in life for good, but it is not all good. Some things are simply evil. For example, it is not good for a little child to die at the hands of anyone, especially his or her parents. Carl Jung said, "The death of a child is putting a period before the end of the sentence."[3]

It is the mystery of God that He allows unspeakable evil. It is the mercy and majesty of God that He can turn even that evil for His good purposes to those who are His deeply loved children.

So, what do we take away from these Scriptures?

The hope that I wrote about in *Study One* is just the beginning. According to Romans 5 we also find our hope grows as we grow. And our growth in character comes about largely through learning to endure and remain steadfast in the face of suffering. And that causes us to rejoice.

We don't rejoice in the pain and suffering itself, but we rejoice in the loving presence of God and the sacred work of God that is taking place in us as the result of that pain and suffering. He is making us like Jesus, conforming us to the image of His Son (Romans 8:29). That strengthens the hope that is within us.

Summing up, we now stand in grace, looking forward to the hope of glory. And we also rejoice in trials that mature us and make us more like Jesus, which serves to amplify our joy and deepen our hope in Christ.

A Pivotal Decision

>> As was said before, we all suffer. No exceptions. The question is whether we will suffer well. Not all will. Suffering doesn't...by itself...guarantee growth and maturity. Suffering without relying on God's grace for strength can easily lead to discouragement, depression, disillusionment, despair and worse. Suffering while trusting in and experiencing God's grace enables us to suffer well, enduring the test and coming out the other side more mature and more like Jesus.

Here are the questions of the hour. It would be really wise to think about how you will answer them in advance of your group meeting and use the blank spaces below to record your thoughts. Then come prepared to honestly discuss this matter in your group. Spend time praying for each other based on how group members respond.

Does your primary purpose and goal in life align with God's great goal for your life? God's design is for you and me to become like Jesus and for us to manifest Him to the world around us. How about you? Is your deepest desire to be wealthy? Comfortable? Admired? Popular? Powerful? Famous? Happy? Entertained? To own the coolest, newest stuff? Have a big home? Big family? An easy life? Or what?

This is your time and place to get honest with God in personally answering these questions:

What I am asking, in essence, is this: *Is it really worth it to follow Christ wholeheartedly, come what may?*

This is a question we all must wrestle with. It is obvious that men like Paul and James believed it was worth it all. But we can't simply piggy-back unthinkingly upon their faith. We have to decide for ourselves.

One more incident from Paul's life will be instructive, then I'll close this study.

Paul had been granted the enormous privilege of seeing what people on earth never see...a glimpse into the very throne room of God in heaven. Who wouldn't want to see that? But seeing what he saw came with a hefty price tag. Was the cost to him worth it? Let's see:

So to keep me from becoming conceited because of the surpassing greatness of the revelations, a thorn was given me in the flesh, a messenger of Satan to harass me, to keep me from becoming conceited. Three times I pleaded with the Lord about this, that it should leave me. But he said to me, 'My grace is sufficient for you, for my power is made perfect in weakness.' Therefore I will boast all the more gladly of my weaknesses, so that the power of Christ may rest upon me. For the sake of Christ, then, I am content with weaknesses, insults, hardships, persecutions, and calamities. For when I am weak, then I am strong.

2 CORINTHIANS 12:7-10

Suffering has a way of deflating (in a good and healthy way) our self-confidence, swagger, and self-reliance, doesn't it? Jesus said that apart from Him we can do nothing (John 15:5), but often in our Christian journeys we don't really believe that. God has to show us by knocking the fleshly wind out of our sails a bit and cutting us down to size. If Paul experienced that, why should we be surprised if we do?

Psalm 119:67 says, *"Before I was afflicted I went astray, but now I keep your word."* God is earnestly, relentlessly and eternally committed to changing our character to be like His Son, the Lord Jesus. It is actually what we were made for. Though he uses everything in life to contribute to this plan, He accelerates the process through suffering. It is God's megaphone.

It reminds me of the story of a father and his young son who strolled into the workshop of a master craftsman. In awe of how realistic this man's carvings of animals were, the father picked up a beautiful carving of an eagle, turning it around and around with admiration. "How in the world do you turn a block of wood into this eagle...a masterpiece of beauty, precision and minute detail?" The craftsman looked up from his work smiling and said, "I just cut away everything that doesn't look like an eagle."

God is committed to cutting away everything in our lives that doesn't look like Jesus. It is painful but the end result is beautiful.

Sounds simple, doesn't it? It is not. It takes the Master Craftsman.

There is still more involved, however, in the Lord's process of how He *unearths* us. Many believe the day is coming when it will be much harder to live as a true disciple of Jesus here in the West than it is now. It is best we be prepared, but to be honest, I don't think we are anywhere close to being ready.

Though it can be a bit unsettling, we need to take a good, hard look at the subject of *persecution*. That is our topic for *Study Four*.

study 4

a blessing in disguise

There are a number of verses in the Bible that I wish weren't there. Maybe you have your "favorites" like that. Thomas Jefferson did. He cut out everything in the New Testament which smacked of the supernatural or miraculous or of Jesus being God. What he was left with was a shorter...much shorter...compilation of our Lord's moral and ethical teachings. Bad move, Mr. Jefferson. You should have read Revelation 22:18,19 before doing that.

I believe he knows better now.

Here are a few verses in the Bible that make me a bit jumpy:

Indeed, all who desire to live a godly life in Christ Jesus will be persecuted, while evil people and impostors will go on from bad to worse, deceiving and being deceived.

2 TIMOTHY 3:12-13

But understand this, that in the last days there will come times of difficulty. For people will be lovers of self, lovers of money, proud, arrogant, abusive, disobedient to their parents, ungrateful, unholy, heartless, unappeasable, slanderous, without self-control, brutal, not loving good, treacherous, reckless, swollen with conceit, lovers of pleasure rather than lovers of God...

2 TIMOTHY 3:1-4

Suffering for Our Faith

The Bible says that suffering for our faith is to be expected and that in the last days prior to Jesus' return, things and people are going to get much worse. And I didn't notice any asterisk in my Bible next to these verses with a footnote saying, "Oh, except in the United States."

That second passage above sounds a lot like the business, political, sports and entertainment sectors of our nation, doesn't it? I think it's quite safe to say that we're living in the "last days."

This study is about persecution.

Persecution has always been part of Church history up to and including the present. And, in many parts of the world, being afflicted for one's faith in Christ is commonplace. It may shock you to realize about 10% of the people in the world who name the Name of Christ live in places where marginalization, discrimination, harassment, violence, imprisonment, torture and even the threat of death are a constant reality[4]. Since it is a much less frequent phenomenon in the West, it is easy to forget that persecution has always been the "Christian norm" rather than the exception.

>> To start this study, it would be interesting to hear from group members if anyone has ever suffered any kind of persecution for their faith. Take some time to talk about those times. Persecution can come from family, friends, neighbors, classmates, fellow employees or elsewhere in one's home country or even abroad. If no one has ever had that experience, that could be pretty convicting, in light of 2 Timothy 3:12,13 above. If that is the case in your group, folks can share things they have heard about or read in books about believers suffering for their faith. Talk about how experiencing (or reading about) that persecution affected your walk with Jesus.

Apart from the reality that persecution has been the companion of the faithful in Christ over the centuries, there is another reality that is worth noting. Persecution, when accompanied by a robust faith in Jesus, disconnects the soul from fleshly and worldly attachments and connects believers closer to the kingdom of God and what awaits us in heaven. In other words, it *unearths* us. What we would likely dread as our greatest challenge in life can actually become one of our greatest allies, a blessing in disguise.

Dr. Josef Tson a Romanian pastor persecuted for his faith later wrote his Ph.D. dissertation on a theology of suffering. In that book, *Suffering, Martyrdom and Rewards in Heaven*, he wrote, "I came to see that whenever the Bible talks about persecution, suffering, and martyrdom, these discussions are always accompanied by promises of great rewards in heaven. I also discovered that the vision of heaven, together with the hope of heavenly rewards, has always been one of the greatest motivations for people facing persecution and martyrdom."[5]

They learned to not forget the glory when the darkness came.

>> Have someone in your group read out loud the words of Jesus from His most famous of all speeches, which we call 'The Sermon on the Mount":

Blessed are those who are persecuted for righteousness' sake, for theirs is the kingdom of heaven. Blessed are you when others revile you and persecute you and utter all kinds of evil against you falsely on my account. Rejoice and be glad, for your reward is great in heaven, for so they persecuted the prophets who were before you.

MATTHEW 5:10-11

>> Then have someone else in your group read these remarkable verses written by the apostle Peter. Discuss together the questions that follow:

Since therefore Christ suffered in the flesh, arm yourselves with the same way of thinking, for whoever has suffered in the flesh has ceased from sin, so as to live for the rest of the time in the flesh no longer for human passions but for the will of God.

1 PETER 4:1-2

>> Here are the questions: *Why did Jesus say that those who endure persecution in His Name are blessed (i.e. exceedingly joyful)? How does our future hope grant strength to endure present day persecution? Does it seem strange to you that the loss of material goods, home, reputation, job, freedom, safety, health, wholeness, family and even life itself for Jesus' sake is something to get excited about? Why or why not? What did Peter mean when he wrote that the effect of suffering in our bodies similar to the way Jesus suffered (through persecution) results in the practice of fleshly sin and human passions somehow being removed from our lives? How is that even possible?*

I am certain that if I were to walk up to the average Christian and tell them I had a surefire secret to finding unbelievable joy, a staggering reward in heaven, and an unprecedented victory over sin on earth, most would practically salivate to hear what I had to say. Wouldn't you? How about now that you know the "secret" involves persecution? I daresay you are probably not drooling.

There is a purifying effect on our souls when we suffer for Jesus. That rings true intuitively. It is hard to imagine someone being imprisoned and beaten for proclaiming the gospel, and then running home to turn on their computer to watch pornography. During the times I have experienced ridicule and injustice for being a witness for Christ, it has accelerated my prayer life and forced me to live more wide-eyed and open-hearted for His kingdom. I can only imagine the multiplication of that effect had I experienced actual physical harm.

Overcoming Fear

It is significant to note that when Jesus sent a very personal letter to seven churches in Asia (see Revelation chapters 2 and 3), there were only two churches to whom He spoke no rebuke nor correction. Both, interestingly enough, were suffering persecution. Here's one of the letters:

And to the angel of the church in Smyrna write: The words of the first and the last, who died and came to life. I know your tribulation and your poverty (but you are rich) and the slander of those who say that they are Jews and are not, but are a synagogue of Satan. Do not fear what you are about to suffer. Behold, the devil is about to throw some of you into prison, that you may be tested, and for ten days you will have tribulation. Be faithful unto death, and I will give you the crown of life. He who has an ear, let him hear what the Spirit says to the churches. The one who conquers will not be hurt by the second death.

REVELATION 2:8-11

What was it that Jesus warned them against? The fear of suffering. The devil (through people he was manipulating) was about to imprison some of the faithful. That was not going to be some country club minimum security prison, by the way. Think dark, dank, filthy, rat-infested, sewage-infected dungeon with little food and little water but lots of chains and beatings.

I think we can take some comfort in reading that these godly folks struggled with the prospect of persecution just like we would. They were afraid. We can also be cheered in knowing that Jesus understood their fear and pointed them to what awaited them in heaven to help them endure. Their responsibility? Don't let fear take over. Hang in there (be faithful) until the end. Jesus knew they could do it and He gave them hope.

Christians have suffered persecution over the centuries. Today in many nations such as North Korea, Eritrea, Somalia, Afghanistan, Pakistan, Syria, Iraq, and Iran believers still suffer terribly.

You may recall the terrorist bombings in Sri Lanka (Easter Sunday, 2019) that killed 254 Christians.[6] Imagine what their families are going through.

Or the thousands of mostly-Christian people from ethnic minorities (Kachin, Karen, Chin peoples) in Myanmar (formerly Burma) who were forced to flee for their lives as a result of brutal airstrikes from the nationalist Buddhist military in the spring, 2018.[7] Their lives have been totally disrupted.

In Saudi Arabia, widely regarded as a Middle Eastern nation friendly to the "Christian" West, it is a capital crime to convert from Islam to Christianity. In some cases, Muslims not wanting to wait for government "justice," have murdered family members who became Christians.[8] Didn't Jesus warn that our enemies could very well be the members of our own household (Matthew 10:36)?

Communist China, with whom the United States has a love-hate trade relationship, has long sought to (and failed to!) halt the spread of Christianity through its brutal harassment, imprisonment and torture of true believers, especially pastors. In fact, the city of Guangzhou has become the first major city in China to offer cash rewards to people ratting on their neighbors who engage in "illegal religious activities." Rewards to these "religious bounty hunters" become even more lucrative if they report the activity of a pastor.[9]

In the 99% Muslim Maldives—a highly regarded tourist destination—a citizen can be jailed for simply owning a Bible.[10]

In July, 2019 a retired Syrian Christian teacher, Suzan Der Kirkour, was repeatedly raped, tortured and stoned to death by extremist Muslim militants. Church members discovered her body near her house in a Christian village. Forensic investigation revealed that her ordeal had lasted nine hours.[11]

Around the world, as many as a quarter of a billion believers in Jesus are under the threat of loss of jobs, home, freedom and family for their faith. Imprisonment, brutal beatings, psychological and physical torture, and the possibility of execution haunt the days of many of our brothers and sisters in Christ.

> It's easy to look at these situations and settle back comfortably in our seemingly safe and secure world. We need to wake up.

Recently a street preacher in London was (unlawfully) arrested, his Bible confiscated and himself driven miles away because someone was offended by his preaching. The officers declared that his preaching was "disturbing people's days." Really? In England?[12]

In the summer of 2019, a Virginia real estate agent was charged with violating fair housing laws because she put John 3:16 on her website, along with phrases like "Jesus loves you." After legal pressure, the Virginia Real Estate Board (VREB) dropped their complaint (they had asserted that her use of religious speech could make someone feel discriminated against). Undaunted, the VREB forced her employer at the time to enter into an agreement to watch her and report back any more religious expression.[13] Creepy.

Add to this the growing number of complaints here in America about crosses and nativity scenes in public places, prayers at high school football games and other harassing complaints and lawsuits, and it is clear that our Western culture is becoming increasingly hostile to people living out their faith in the public arena. How long until preaching the gospel and naming sin become illegal "hate speech"?

>> What about you? How do you respond to these potential threats to our freedom of speech and freedom of religion? Below I have created a "Fear Forecast" evaluation tool. Put a mark below in the continuum of anxiety that you feel toward the potential of experiencing persecution in each area. How would experiencing persecution affect your willingness and boldness to tell others about Jesus? Persecution doesn't come to those who hide their faith; it is launched against those who are outspoken. The devil brings the threat of persecution to try and keep our mouths shut about Jesus.

It would be best to fill this out in advance of your meeting when you have unhurried time. Then, when you gather in your group, talk about these issues.

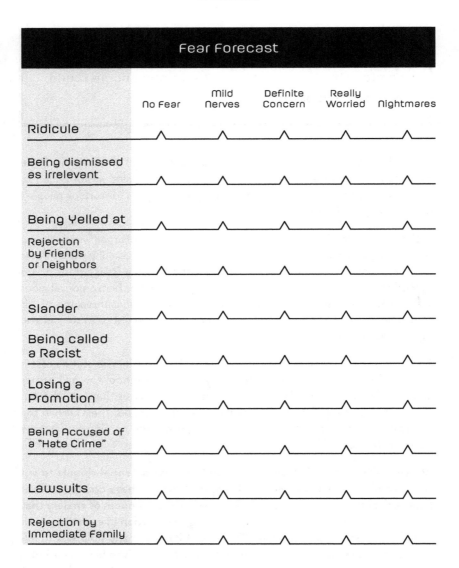

Fear Forecast

	No Fear	Mild Nerves	Definite Concern	Really Worried	Nightmares
Ridicule					
Being dismissed as irrelevant					
Being Yelled at					
Rejection by Friends or Neighbors					
Slander					
Being called a Racist					
Losing a Promotion					
Being Accused of a "Hate Crime"					
Lawsuits					
Rejection by Immediate Family					

>> After your discussion, take some time during your group meeting to spread out, get alone with God and talk with Him about what He has shown you in the exercise above. So much of what we fear will happen to us is a mirage of deception planted in our minds by the enemy of our souls. To listen to and obey these fears is to cease to walk by faith. And whatever is not of faith, is sin (Romans 14:23). Proverbs 28:1 says, "The wicked flee when no one pursues, but the righteous are bold as a lion." Use the following prayer as a guide for this time of personal repentance.

PRAYER OF REPENTANCE

Dear heavenly Father, Your Son, the Lord Jesus, did not want to go through the suffering of the Cross and yet He said, "Not my will, but Yours be done." In my humanity, I acknowledge that fear has often held me back from doing Your will. Too often I have done my will and not Yours. At times I have chosen not to open my mouth and talk about my faith in Jesus for fear of a negative reaction from people. Please forgive me for my disobedience to You and for giving in to fear. As I look over the list of ways persecution is possible here in the West, I am convicted of how fear has kept me from speaking out and boldly proclaiming Jesus. Specifically, I confess and renounce the fear(s) of (list the fears that came to light in the exercise above). Thank You so much for Your forgiveness. I am sorry that my aversion to discomfort and dislike of awkward or confrontational situations have kept me from telling others about Jesus. I recognize this as selfish and unloving by withholding such great news to people that are without Jesus and therefore without hope and without God in this world. I reject fear and claim the "power, love and a sound mind" that are mine in Christ (2 Timothy 1:7). Set me free from all my fears, Lord Jesus, and grant me boldness by Your Holy Spirit to be Your faithful witness (Acts 1:8). Amen.

The Power of Prayer

In addition to renouncing our fear and seeking God's empowerment to be His bold witness, there is more that we can do in the face of persecution.

Remember those who are in prison as though in prison with them, and those who are mistreated, since you are also in the body.

HEBREWS 13:3

You likely attend a church where week after week, year after year, you have complete freedom to worship Jesus, read from the Bible, hear a fully biblical sermon, sing praises to God at the top of your lungs and pray out loud...all without the slightest risk of persecution. This truly is freedom of religion and we are often guilty of taking it for granted. I know I am. Many, many brothers and sisters in Christ around the world can only dream of such liberty.

How can we help those who are being persecuted and imprisoned for the sake of Christ in our world?

Dr. Nik Ripken (not his real name), in his profoundly eye-opening book, *The Insanity of God*, wrote of an incident he witnessed with former Muslims who were experiencing persecution as believers in Christ. These new converts from Islam were expressing their deep gratitude to God, yearning to one day travel to China to personally thank the multitude of believers there who had been praying for these ex-Muslims to remain strong in their new faith in Jesus.[14]

Remarkably, many of those in the persecuted Church pray for us in the West, knowing how hard it is for the rich "not to set their hopes on the uncertainty of riches but on God" (1 Timothy 6:17). They know that we face a far greater peril than even persecution.

> There is the very real danger that in all our peace and affluence we might simply forget God.

That has already occurred. But God, in His wisdom, will answer the prayers of the remnant who cry out for revival in the West. God uses persecution to stir the pot, fan the flames, and purify His Church. It will work, but it will not be easy.

In the West, since we rarely suffer for our faith as the godly people in the New Testament did and as saints in other parts of the world do, we may be tempted to glamorize persecution.

Let's be real. There is nothing glamorous about persecution. It is awful and brings about great misery. And it is dangerous. Not all who suffer for their faith survive or even stay steadfast in Christ. The apostle Paul was aware of the peril of persecution when he wrote:

> ***Therefore when we could bear it no longer, we were willing to be left behind in Athens alone, and we sent Timothy, our brother and God's coworker in the gospel of Christ, to establish you and exhort you in your faith, that no one be swayed by these afflictions. For you yourselves know that we were destined for this. For when we were with you, we kept telling you beforehand that we were to suffer affliction, just as it has come to pass, and just as you know. For this reason, when I could bear it no longer, I sent to learn about your faith, for fear that somehow the tempter had tempted you and our labor would be in vain.***
>
> 1 THESSALONIANS 3:1-5

It would be a tragedy if we forgot these precious family members in Christ who are grievously suffering for their faith around the world. They need our help. Prayer is one way of remembering those in prison for their faith.

>> I suggest that those in your group boldly pray the following prayer together out loud, utilizing your religious freedom to publicly come alongside those who do not have such freedom:

PRAY

Dear heavenly Father, I confess that I have been largely unaware of what is going on with 10% of my brothers and sisters in Christ around the world who are suffering today for their bold and uncompromising faith in You. Please forgive me for neglecting to help them and for taking for granted the great freedom to worship You that I have. Open my eyes to the needs of believers who have been imprisoned and mistreated for their faith. Grant me the wisdom of finding practical ways to help. For now, I pray for them. You know their names and the names of their family members, Lord, and what they are going through. Would you please comfort them and, in Your mercy, provide their daily bread and sufficient clothing to keep them warm? Please grant them strength to endure difficult circumstances and the pain that I can't even imagine. Keep my heart from becoming ungrateful, calloused and unmoved by their plight. Cause me to weep with those who weep. Enable them to experience Your presence and know Your deep peace despite their hardship. Grant them grace to even love their enemies and pray for the salvation of their captors and torturers. I don't come to You in my own name, but I come in Your great Name, Jesus. You see them, are with them, and You know just what to do to sustain them. Bless them with a sure, steadfast and unwavering faith to know that You are there and will never forsake them. Remind them today that this world is not all there is. Give them the full assurance of the hope of eternal life. Amen.

Living Courageously in Christ

Courageous faith has always been a mark of godly people. Shadrach, Meshach and Abednego made the brave choice not to worship a golden idol in Babylon, even though it meant the likelihood of being incinerated (Daniel 3). Jeremiah was chucked into a horrible, mucky slime pit of a cistern for boldly proclaiming truth (Jeremiah 38). Hebrews 11 lists hero after hero of the faith, many of whom suffered greatly for their steadfastness of belief. That chapter climaxes with a crescendo of accolades for those who we will be privileged to meet one day in heaven.

>> Have someone in your group read Hebrews 11:32-39 out loud, then discuss the following questions together:

What are some of the great exploits of courage that the writer of Hebrews mentions in these verses? Which Old Testament stories of bravery for God impress you the most? Why? Not all of the incidents listed here are "success stories." What were some of the sufferings these great saints had to endure? Why did the writer of Hebrews insert the phrase, "of whom the world was not worthy"? What did he mean by that?

It encourages me to know that the Hall of Faith in Hebrews 11 is still open for new inductees in our day.

A number of years ago I had the privilege of attending the Deeper Walk International biennial conference in Indianapolis, IN. The keynote speaker was Pastor Josef Tson, who I mentioned earlier in this study. Josef pastored in Romania when his nation was under Communist rule and was imprisoned numerous times for his faith as the government sought vainly to silence him. He was eventually exiled from Romania in 1981 and returned there in 1991 to serve Christ after Communism fell.

At that conference, Josef recounted a conversation in prison with the man who was (at that time) the cruelest and most notorious torturer of believers in Romania. This is basically what Josef said to that man:

> *"Here is how this works. Your greatest weapon is to kill me. My greatest weapon is to die. If I die, all my books and recordings will become 10 times more powerful for Jesus to use since my martyr's blood will be sprinkled all over them. People will want to get them even more."*

The humorous epilogue to that story was that the cruel torturer dude later spoke about Josef with another imprisoned pastor. He said, "Josef wants us to kill him, but we are not going to!"

How do you stop a man with that kind of faith? You can't. Because of Josef's rock-solid confidence in God and hope in Jesus, he became essentially invincible.

The apostle Paul paved the way for such indomitable faith centuries earlier when he wrote:

Only let your manner of life be worthy of the gospel of Christ, so that whether I come and see you or am absent, I may hear of you that you are standing firm in one spirit, with one mind striving side by side for the faith of the gospel, and not frightened in anything by your opponents. This is a clear sign to them of their destruction, but of your salvation, and that from God. For it has been granted to you that for the sake of Christ you should not only believe in him but also suffer for his sake.

PHILIPPIANS 1:27-29

>> In your groups, discuss what both the apostle Paul and Josef said. It is important to realize that Josef had undergone numerous imprisonments with very harsh "brainwashing" and physical beatings. His courage was not naïve bravado, but battle-tested faith. We have already looked at some of what Paul went through in our previous study. How does one come to the place of full and genuine surrender and courage that these men achieved?

Then have someone read the following Scriptures out loud and discuss the questions that follow:

Beloved, do not be surprised at the fiery trial when it comes upon you to test you, as though something strange were happening to you. But rejoice insofar as you share Christ's sufferings, that you may also rejoice and be glad when his glory is revealed. If you are insulted for the name of Christ, you are blessed, because the Spirit of glory and of God rests on you.

1 PETER 4:12-14

And I heard a loud voice in heaven, saying, 'Now the salvation and the power and the kingdom of our God and the authority of Christ have come, for the accuser of our brothers has been thrown down, who accuses them day and night before our God. And they have conquered him by the blood of the Lamb and by the word of their testimony, for they loved not their lives even unto death.

REVELATION 12:10-11

Who shall separate us from the love of Christ? Shall tribulation, or distress, or persecution, or famine, or nakedness, or danger, of sword? As it is written, 'For your sake we are being killed all the day long; we are regarded as sheep to be slaughtered.' No, in all these things we are more than conquerors through him who loved us.

ROMANS 8:35-37

>> Questions: Should we be shocked and caught off guard when persecution comes our way? Why or why not? Why should we greet such trials with joy and gladness? What do you think it means to have "the Spirit of glory and of God" resting on you? What are the three "weapons" that are needed to conquer Satan, according to Revelation 12? Are you equipped with all three? Death seems like a defeat. How can it be that even while dying for Christ, the believer is still "more than a conqueror"?

In his book, Pastor Richard Wurmbrand (also Romanian) tells story after story of the beauty and heroism of the saints who suffered almost unimaginable brutality at the hands of the Communists. That book, *Tortured for Christ*, is a must-read for all who long for a vital, indomitable faith in these last days. Here are just a couple of excerpts from that book:

> *"I was later in prison together with souls whom God had helped me to win for Christ. I was in the same cell with one who had left behind six children and who was now in prison for his Christian faith. His wife and children were starving. He might never see them again. I asked him, 'Have you any resentment against me that I brought you to Christ and because of this your family is in such misery?' He answered, 'I have no words to express my thankfulness that you have brought me to this wonderful Savior. I would never have it any other way.'"*[15]

One of Wurmbrand's conclusions (after going through 14 years of cruel incarceration for his faith) could only have been learned through persecution. He learned that *"physical beatings could be endured, and that the human spirit with God's help can survive horrible tortures."*[16]

I don't know about you, but that is just what I need to hear.

> Suffering does not have to win. Pain doesn't have the last word. Cruelty need not break the human spirit. There is grace to endure to the end, and an eternity beyond this life where suffering becomes a distant memory.

Do you yearn for a faith like that? Here's another story from Pastor Wurmbrand to galvanize your spiritual backbone:

> *"The following scene happened more times than I can remember. A brother was preaching to the other prisoners when the guards suddenly burst in, surprising him halfway through a phrase. They hauled him down the corridor to their 'beating room.' After what seemed an endless beating, they brought him back and threw him—bloody and bruised—on the prison floor. Slowly, he picked up his battered body, painfully straightened his clothing and said, 'Now, brethren, where did I leave off when I was interrupted?' He continued his gospel message."*[17]

Why do I include these stories? To scare you? No, but to strengthen your faith so that you know at a heart level that no matter what may be down the road for believers in the West, with God's help we can endure. Yes, and even rejoice. We can be courageous.

Early on in the life of the Church, the apostles were arrested for preaching the good news. They boldly witnessed for Christ to the religious leaders who were beside themselves with rage, not knowing what to do with them. The crowds were eating up what Peter, John and company had to say, so a wise man, Gamaliel, urged the leaders to be careful. They took his advice.

>> Go ahead and have someone in your group read the following Scripture out loud:

And when they had called in the apostles, they beat them and charged them not to speak in the name of Jesus, and let them go. Then they left the presence of the council, rejoicing that they were counted worthy to suffer dishonor for the name. And every day, in the temple and from house to house, they did not cease teaching and preaching that the Christ is Jesus.

ACTS 5:40-42

>> Discuss the following questions together: In what specific ways did the apostles experience persecution? We can assume Peter was one of these apostles. How was Peter able to triumph in this circumstance when not long before he had denied Jesus three times? What was the end result of this incident of persecution? Did it accomplish what the persecutors intended for it to do?

The disciples had never directly experienced suffering like this. They had watched Jesus arrested and Peter had been so scared of suffering the same fate that he denied the Lord three times. How would they respond when persecution came upon them? Since grace is not given in advance of the need, they couldn't know until it happened. And they responded with joy, feeling honored to suffer dishonor in Jesus' name. And they kept right on preaching.

What had changed for Peter and the apostles? First, they had seen the risen Lord Jesus. Second, they were filled with the Holy Spirit. No longer defeated and despondent, they were inflamed and energized with the mighty resurrection power of God.

That strengthens my hope that if ever I were forced to endure real deprivation, physical beatings, imprisonment or even death, I would find God's grace sufficient just as the apostles did. You and I can be filled with the Holy Spirit, just as they were!

I hope you are encouraged as well.

Loving Our Enemies

This final section deserves a whole book, but time and space allow us only a brief glance before I close this study. You have probably rolled your eyeballs and sighed a bit when reading these words of Jesus:

But I say to you who hear, Love your enemies, do good to those who hate you, bless those who curse you, pray for those who abuse you...But love your enemies, and do good and lend, expecting nothing in return, and your reward will be great, and you will be sons of the Most High, for he is kind to the ungrateful and the evil. Be merciful, even as your Father is merciful.

LUKE 6:27-28, 35-36

If we were ever under the delusion that somehow, in our own strength, we could live the Christian life, these verses should instantly shatter that silly mirage in our minds.

Loving our enemies? Really? Praying even for those who would torture us? Has Jesus gone mad? As crazy and unrealistic as this sounds, these words are as much the truth-teaching of Jesus as the verses we like to quote, like John 3:16, John 11:25,26 and others. Again, I turn to the remarkable stories from Pastor Wurmbrand to reassure us that what Jesus commands us to do He will also empower us to do through the Holy Spirit:

> *"When one Christian was sentenced to death, he was allowed to see his wife before being executed. His last words to his wife were: 'You must know that I die loving those who kill me. They don't know what they do and my last request of you is to love them, too. Don't have bitterness in your heart because they killed your beloved one. We will meet in heaven.' These words impressed the officer of the secret police who attended the discussion between the two. He later told me the story in prison where he had been sent for becoming a Christian."*[18]

> *"A minister who had been horribly beaten was thrown into my cell. He was half-dead, with blood streaming from his face and body. We washed him. Some prisoners cursed the Communists. Groaning, he said, 'Please don't curse them! Keep silent! I wish to pray for them."*[19]

Some of Pastor Wurmbrand's final comments in his book will not leave me alone, they are so riveting:

> *"It was in prison that we found the hope of salvation for the Communists. It was there that we developed a sense of responsibility toward them. It was in being tortured by them that we learned to love them."*[20]

I encourage all of you in your group to pray the following prayer out loud together as you conclude this study:

PRAY

Father in heaven, this study has challenged me to the core. There are levels of surrender, faith, growth, freedom and maturity in Christ that seem light years beyond my ability to ever attain. It encourages me to know that You accept me just the way I am, even as I wrestle with the world, flesh and devil as they seek to keep me stuck in this place. Knowing the incredible hope that awaits me in heaven and the relative shortness of my stay here on earth, I ask that You would transform me as my mind is renewed. Give me the mindset of the early disciples and the brave saints around the world who do not love their lives even unto death. Please fill me with the Holy Spirit. Whatever it takes, whatever you need to bring my way, please grant me grace to accept it with joy, that I might be Your bold and uncompromising witness. When my life is all said and done, may the mighty Name of the Lord Jesus Christ have been greatly honored and glorified. And in that Name I pray, amen.

study 5

mercy and mystery

Despite being situated almost halfway through our Bible, most scholars believe that *Job* was actually the first book of the Old Testament written. Interesting, isn't it? The oldest biblical writing is about suffering. Perhaps that is because the burning questions of *"How can a good God allow suffering to good people?"* and *"Where is God in the midst of my pain?"* have been universally asked since the beginning of time.

Job's brutal honesty in the midst of his torment serves as a great role model for all sufferers, as he seeks to figure out where God is in the midst of it all. The book also gives insights how to minister to, and especially how *not* to minister to someone who is going through trials.

The book of *Job* opens with a two-chapter prologue that takes place in heaven and which allows us to eavesdrop on conversations between God and Satan. God initiates this dialogue.

It all starts when God points Satan to Job's righteous life. Satan scoffs at Job, believing it is only because God coddles him that Job trusts Him. Satan dares God to remove the hedge of protection around Job and to shatter his secure world. As all heaven awaits in hushed silence for God's response, the Lord astonishingly accepts the devil's dare.

Gleefully, I'm sure, the devil goes off and does his thing to Job and his family. You get the distinct impression that God had this whole thing planned way in advance.

Thus begins a cosmic showdown to see if man will worship God just for who He is and not for what He does for us.

It is helpful to observe that God was totally in charge of the situation and the devil could only do to Job what God allowed him to do. God is sovereign. The devil is always on a leash, so to speak. But there is something else that we need to know about Job's suffering.

Though the reader is very aware of why Job is going through such intense pain and suffering, it is evident from the book that Job himself is unaware of why all this is happening to him.

Job had no clue that his life was on display before all the angels (good and bad) and that one day a book written about his suffering would serve to encourage millions of people throughout history. Psychologists or sociologists would call it a "blind" or "blinded experiment."

The absence of any warning to Job of impending disaster as well as a lack of any explanation by God as to the reason for his suffering is so true to life for us today, isn't it? Usually we don't know why we go through trials either. Sometimes it seems so pointless. Job certainly felt that way.

A brief sampling from Job's complaint illustrates his pain and frustration at God's lack of explanation as well as His (seeming) absence:

Today also my complaint is bitter; my hand is heavy on account of my groaning. Oh, that I knew where I might find him, that I might come even to his seat! I would lay my case before him and fill my mouth with arguments...Would he contend with me in the greatness of his power? No; he would pay attention to me...Behold, I go forward, but he is not there, and backward, but I do not perceive him; on the left hand when he is working, I do not behold him; he turns to the right hand, but I do not see him.

JOB 23:2-4, 6, 8-9

The Burning Questions

>> As we open up this discussion about discovering God in the midst of pain, take some time to talk about this issue in your group, discussing the following questions:

Have you ever experienced pain and wondered where God was in the midst of it? Have you ever struggled with wondering why God allowed (or is allowing)

you to suffer so much? Did you ever cry out to God in the midst of some difficult situation and all you received in response was dead silence?

Talk about those times honestly in your group, making sure to express how you felt (or feel) toward God as a result of that suffering. Don't be afraid to be totally transparent; God can take it and He already knows what you are feeling anyway. Our emotions do not surprise or shock God at all.

Job was not the only one in Scripture to struggle with the perceived absence of God in the midst of suffering. There were many others. For example, King David wrote:

> *How long, O LORD? Will you forget me forever? How long will you hide your face from me? How long must I take counsel in my soul and have sorrow in my heart all the day? How long shall my enemy be exalted over me?*
>
> PSALM 13:1-2

The question, *"How long...?"* indicates pain that seems unrelenting and unending. Our situation can seem hopeless; we fear things will never get better. It is very possible that, in the midst of chronic suffering, the powers of darkness can overwhelm us and bring us to despair. Suicide may even seem like the only way out. David appeared to be aware of the danger he was in:

> *Consider and answer me, O LORD my God; light up my eyes, lest I sleep the sleep of death, lest my enemy say, 'I have prevailed over him,' lest my foes rejoice because I am shaken.*
>
> PSALM 13:3-4

It is instructive to realize that David continued to pray during his suffering. He did not turn away from God and shut Him out. Though there are no clear indications that David's circumstances changed as he wrote this psalm, he comes to a life-altering conclusion:

But I have trusted in your steadfast love; my heart shall rejoice in your salvation. I will sing to the LORD, because he has dealt bountifully with me.

PSALM 13:56

David was able to rejoice in God and even sing to Him because a) he chose to trust in God's love that he knew would never quit on him and b) he had hope in the LORD's future deliverance that he knew would one day come.

Can God Be Trusted?

>> Just like David, we are going to take a look at some of the attributes of God that will stabilize our souls in the midst of suffering. As before, I urge you to complete this assignment prior to your meeting. Then you will be prepared to discuss this together.

Below you will find five attributes of God that are particularly relevant when our journey with Christ brings us over rough terrain. Each attribute is accompanied by at least one Scripture, though there are many others that could have been selected.

What God says in His Word is unequivocally true, but often that truth fails to move from intellectual understanding to heart conviction. This exercise is designed to help bridge that gap. After each attribute and Scripture, you will be asked to write a statement that personalizes and applies that quality of God's character to a time when you were suffering. There is an example given so you get the idea.

God's presence (there is no place I can go where God is not there)

"Where shall I go from your Spirit? Or where shall I flee from your presence? If I ascend to heaven, you are there! If I make my bed in Sheol, you are there! If I take the wings of the morning and dwell in the uttermost parts of the sea, even there your hand shall lead me, and your right hand shall hold me." (Psalm 139:7-10)

Personalized application (example): When I was suffering so badly from the effects of the chemo, there was never a moment when You, God, were not there with me, holding me.

Now write your own: ______________________________

____

____

____

God's goodness (God's motivations, intentions and actions are always to provide the best for me)

"And I will make an everlasting covenant with them; I will never stop doing good for them. I will put a desire in their hearts to worship me, and they will never leave me." (Jeremiah 32:40 NLT)

Personalized Application: __________________________

____

____

____

God's faithful, never-failing care for His children (He is always alert, aware and attentive to me all my life)

"For you formed my inward parts; you knitted me together in my mother's womb. I praise you for I am fearfully and wonderfully made. Wonderful are your works; my soul knows it very well. My frame was not hidden from you, when I was being made in secret, intricately woven in the depths of the earth. Your eyes saw my unformed substance; in your book were written, every one of them, the days that were formed for me, when as yet there was none of them. How precious to me are your thoughts, O God! How vast is the sum of them! If I would count them, they are more than the sand. I awake, and I am still with you." (Psalm 139:13-18)

Personalized Application: __________________________

____

____

____

God's mighty power (He is able to do all that He purposes to do; His strength knows no limits)

"Ah, Lord GOD! It is you who have made the heavens and the earth by your great power and by your outstretched arm! Nothing is too hard for you." (Jeremiah 32:17)

"The word of the LORD came to Jeremiah: 'Behold, I am the LORD, the God of all flesh. Is anything too hard for me?" (Jeremiah 32:26-27)

Personalized Application: ______________________________

____

____

____

God's mercy (He will never stop being warm, tender, caring and compassionate to us; He is never cruel, arbitrary or cold)

"Remember my affliction and my wanderings, the wormwood and the gall! My soul continually remembers it and is bowed down within me. But this I call to mind, and therefore I have hope: The steadfast love of the LORD never ceases; his mercies never come to an end; they are new every morning; great is your faithfulness. 'The LORD is my portion,' says my soul, 'therefore I will hope in him.'" (Lamentations 3:19-24)

Personalized Application: ______________________________

____

____

____

Our hope in God and core trust in His character is "a sure and steadfast anchor of the soul" (Hebrews 6:19). God is real, alive and unchanging. He is the same yesterday, today and forever (Hebrews 13:8).

> The truth of who God is, however, must be married to our faith in Him. If we don't know the truth and if we don't believe the truth, the truth will do us no good.

If you are still struggling with finding the place of trust and rest in Him, I encourage you to continue prayerfully thinking about the Scriptures above (and any others you find helpful).

But, as this study's title suggests, there is another element of God that we must understand and accept if we are to have peace of mind and heart in any and every circumstance.

The Mystery of God

We must embrace not only the mercy but also the mystery of God.

God's Word provides a good starting point to understand what this means for us:

> ***For my thoughts are not your thoughts, neither are your ways my ways, declares the LORD. For as the heavens are higher than the earth, so are my ways higher than your ways and my thoughts than your thoughts.***
> ISAIAH 55:8-9

As I taught in *unstuck*, it doesn't take long as a new Christian to notice that the way God thinks and the way God does things are different from the way we think and do things. But it takes faith to believe that His thoughts and ways are not only *different*, but *higher*. That is, God's ways and thoughts are purer, smarter, wiser, and holier than ours. In short, they are *better*. By a long shot. It's not even close.

Every time we think we know better than God what should be done or how it should be done, we are wrong. That kicks our pride in the gut and we don't like that. But think about it: Should it surprise us to find that our Father knows better than we do how to run the universe and guide our lives? After all, He is God and we are not.

Part of the way God runs the universe and leads our lives is in choosing not to answer all our questions. He lets us in on a lot of things, but not on all things. Scripture says:

The secret things belong to the LORD our God, but the things that are revealed belong to us and to our children forever, that we may do all the words of this law.
DEUTERONOMY 29:29

God is very open to us. He has revealed a tremendous amount about Himself, ourselves and how to live life in obedience to His Word. But He hasn't pulled the curtain back on everything. That is by design. He knows that there is only so much that we...in our current fallen condition...can grasp. The rest must wait.

Alaine Pakkala of *Lydia Discipleship Ministries* has tremendous insight into this area of trusting God in the midst of suffering. Herself a glorious survivor of Satanic Ritual Abuse (SRA), she has a ministry of discipleship to the most broken and shattered in the body of Christ. Her answers to my many questions provided much help for this chapter.

Alaine warns that there are traps we can fall into that rob us of embracing and trusting God in our pain and which can even lead to despair. Here are six of those dangers:

- We neglect daily feeding on the Word of God and so have little basis for faith.
- We disbelieve in God's willingness or ability to speak to us so we share very little in the way of intimacy with Him.
- We believe the devil's lies that we deserve all the pain and suffering we are experiencing and think God is punishing us.
- We believe we deserve an easy life and when things get tough and don't go the way we planned, we are indignant or even outraged, thinking God is unfair.
- We expect God to always heal and deliver when we "take dominion" or "stand in our authority" and if nothing happens, we blame it on the victim's lack of faith.
- We demand an explanation from God as to why He is allowing our suffering and believe we are entitled to know. Only if we receive an explanation that makes sense to us do we deem God worthy of our trust.

>> In your groups, take some time to look over those six dangers. Discuss what happens to us and our relationship with God if we are trapped in these practices or beliefs. Then talk about which of them you are most likely to struggle with and why. Conclude this discussion by praying for one another that the Lord would have His way to make any needed adjustments to your attitude or actions.

I have taken theology courses and found them helpful. There is value in theology, but if our theology does not leave any "wiggle room" for the mystery of God, to that degree it is unhelpful and even harmful.

> We dare not think we have God all figured out. That is arrogance. We need to come to the point of joyfully admitting, "I don't know everything and I don't understand it all, but He does."

Job's three "friends" had a theology that basically said, "If you are a good boy, good things will happen to you. But the fact you are experiencing bad things, Job, means you have somehow been a bad boy." That cold, sterile, formulaic approach to understanding suffering was unfair to Job and severely displeasing to God. It was only Job's prayers for those three jokers that spared them from God's burning anger (see Job 42:7-9).

Can we come to the place of accepting that there are some things we are incapable of understanding and when God doesn't answer the demands of our "Why?" questions, that He is not being difficult or unreasonable?

Is it also not possible, at times when we strain in vain to hear anything from God, that perhaps He isn't being silent at all? Could He be speaking, but not in the way we expect?

Just because God seems silent
doesn't mean He isn't communicating in other ways
or that He is absent, aloof or uncaring.

Consider this: The most powerful thing we can do with people who suffer is to just be with them. Even Job's friends got that right for seven days. Then they started talking and it was all over.

Which would you rather have when you are going through pain: Someone who shows up and yammers on, trying to explain all the reasons why you are going through this affliction, or someone who sits quietly with you, with his/her arm around your shoulder, weeping with you?

Scripture speaks of God, saying:

In all their distress he too was distressed and the angel of his presence saved them. In his love and mercy he redeemed them; he lifted them up and carried them all the days of old.

ISAIAH 63:9

God is not emotionally aloof. Jesus wept at the tomb of Lazarus (John 11:35) and He weeps with us as well. God also speaks to us and comforts us by His faithful presence and the kindness of His children who know enough to be still and know that He is God. Maybe we need to learn to compose and quiet our souls before Him, letting Him minister as only He can, rather than expecting Him to do things our way.

Before closing this study and shifting gears into the final portions of unearthed, there is one more element to the mystery of God with which we must grapple:

This element of mystery involves the realities of **choice** and **time**.

When we look at all the evil that is in the world, we can't help but notice that God gives a lot of leeway for people to choose wickedness, if they are so inclined. That is, there is a dignity allotted to the human race, fallen as it is. And part of that dignity is the moral responsibility to choose right over wrong rather than be forced by God into submission to do His will.

The Bible paints a very real picture of the activity of men who have chosen evil:

He says in his heart, 'I shall not be moved; throughout all generations I shall not meet adversity.' His mouth is filled with cursing and deceit and oppression; under his tongue are mischief and iniquity. He sits in ambush in the villages; in hiding places he murders the innocent. His eyes stealthily watch for the helpless; he lurks

in ambush like a lion in his thicket; he lurks that he may seize the poor; he seizes the poor when he draws him into his net. The helpless are crushed, sink down, and fall by his might. He says in his heart, 'God has forgotten, he has hidden his face, he will never see it.'

PSALM 10:6-11

When we read passages of Scripture like this, it is human nature to cry out, "Why doesn't God simply put a stop to wickedness? Why does He allow it to go on for so long? Why does evil seem so often to win?"

It is clear that God has chosen not to intervene and simply stop all the evil in the world from happening...at least not yet.

Sometimes He does prevent evil, for which we are deeply grateful. We rejoice when we hear on the news how a plot by a student to shoot up his school was discovered by police ahead of time and derailed before anyone got hurt. Or how brave firefighters rescued a family from their burning home with no serious injuries.

Who can ever forget the rescue in 2010 of the 33 Chilean miners trapped 2300 feet underground for 69 days? Every one of them made it to the surface safely! Or the drama of the Thai boys' soccer team in 2018, when unbelievably all made it out alive (12 kids and their coach) after being trapped in a flooded cave for 18 days?

We give honor and glory to God for such mercy. And rightfully so!

But many times, God doesn't stop the evil. He doesn't magically turn bullets into bubbles as they burst from the barrel of an AR-15 assault rifle. The Holocaust happened. So did oppression under Stalin and Pol Pot and Mao and...the list is endless.

In our own country, the Civil War took place. More recently, God did not divert the commercial airliners away from the World Trade Center on 9/11. He did not blow all the toxic ash away from the fleeing populace in Manhattan nor prevent the first responders from being crushed by the falling buildings.

The nation of Israel suffered grievously under the slave drivers of Egypt for 400 years before God sent Moses as their deliverer. 400 years? That's way longer than the entire lifetime of the United States of America.

What is up with all this?

God certainly views time differently than we do. It seems like forever since Jesus walked on planet Earth, but not to God:

But do not overlook this one fact, beloved, that with the Lord one day is as a thousand years, and a thousand years as one day. The Lord is not slow to fulfill his promise as some count slowness, but is patient toward you, not wishing that any should perish, but that all should reach repentance.
2 PETER 3:8-9

It is a short step from believing God is dragging His heels and taking way too long to rescue us, to concluding that He is not good.

Ever since the Garden of Eden, the devil has tried to undermine mankind's faith in the goodness of God. Remember his first question to Eve:

Did God actually say, 'You shall not eat of any tree in the garden?'
GENESIS 3:1B

The insinuation to Eve was that God was stingy, cruel and was withholding good things from her. In other words, "God is not good." The devil's relentless assault on the goodness of God has ferociously battered the human heart ever since.

But the devil is a liar (John 8:44) and the truth is that God is good. Scripture says:

The LORD is gracious and merciful, slow to anger and abounding in steadfast love. The LORD is good to all, and his mercy is over all that he has made...The LORD is righteous in all his ways and kind in all his works.
PSALM 145:8-9,17

The Test of Trusting God

God, in His goodness, doesn't always prevent evil but He does preserve His people in the midst of it. Even when death is the result of that evil, death does not have the last word for the people of God. And when evil and suffering linger longer than we had ever dreaded, God's sustaining grace perseveres through to the end.

Our trust in God must somehow find room for the mystery of not only the presence of evil and suffering in the world (by God's allowance of man's choice), but also its persistence over time. This is not an easy test to pass. Pain can tear the heart out of trust, especially when it just won't quit.

There are three directions we can take in facing these tough issues of the mystery of God:

- We can bury our heads in the sand and pretend these challenges to faith don't exist
- We can become bitter and put God on trial in our hearts and find Him guilty as charged
- We can humble ourselves and admit that we simply do not know the answers to these mysteries but that God has revealed Himself as good, and for now, that is enough

The first option is the coward's way out and will never allow us to fully grow up in Christ.

The second option is the defiant rebel's way out and leads only to despair.

The third option is the way of faith, recognizing that God never consulted with us as to how He should run things anyway, and that He has yet to bring about the final chapter of the story.

>> In this next discussion, address the following questions: What thoughts do you have concerning this element of God's mystery (choice and time)? What troubles you? What reassures you of God's goodness? Which of the three options above will you choose? Why?

After finishing your discussion, I invite you to join together in prayer, out loud:

PRAY

Dear heavenly Father, I remember when Jesus preached a sermon that was really hard for the people to hear. Most of His disciples left at that time. Your Son, the

Lord Jesus, then asked the apostles if they were going to leave also. Peter spoke up and said, "Lord, to whom shall we go? You have the words of eternal life, and we have believed, and have come to know, that you are the Holy One of God" (John 6:68,69). This is kind of like that moment. Part of the great dignity You have afforded the human race is the privilege of choice. So, at this moment, even with all my questions far from answered, I choose You. Amen.

Alaine Pakkala, when she was an 8-year-old girl, was confronted by her abusers who mockingly said, "Why don't you call on your God to stop us from what we are about to do to you?" Alaine prayed and the terrible abuse happened anyway. Mocking her faith and the seeming disinterest toward or impotence of God against their wickedness, Alaine responded in the midst of her confused pain:

> *"Even though my God did not stop you, I still choose Him."*[21]

Kind of sounds like Job, doesn't it: *"Though he slay me, yet will I trust in him."* (Job 13:15 KJV)

Fifteen years later, God chose to give Alaine a response to her child-like questions about that incident. He reassured her that He had heard all her prayers. He comforted her by telling her that every time she wept, He wept with her. He also made it clear that she just wasn't capable in this life of understanding it all. But His final words to her were the most poignant:

> *"Do you trust Me?"*[22]

She said "yes." Will we?

>> Before concluding this study, take a few minutes in your group to allow members to talk about times in their lives when they were able to trust God even when things seemed dark. How were they able to make that choice of faith? Are they able to look back and see how their trust in God was vindicated? If not, how are they able to persevere in trusting God anyway?

Jesus said: "And will not God give justice to his elect, who cry to him day and night? Will he delay long over them? I tell you, he will give justice to them speedily. Nevertheless, when the Son of Man comes, will he find faith on earth?"

LUKE 18:7-8

Every heroic story has tension, a suspense-filled drama that remains unresolved until the very end. We are not at the end yet. But Jesus spoke crucial words of encouragement to His disciples and to us when He said:

I have told you all this so that you may have peace in me. Here on earth you will have many trials and sorrows. But take heart, because I have overcome the world.

JOHN 16:33 NLT

Right now, we do not see the fulfillment of Jesus' victory over a hostile world. Jesus' words, however, could not be truer. For now, we must hang onto this truth.

There will indeed come a day when our Lord roars from heaven: "Enough!" and all things will be made new. As we wait, we can be filled with hope as we look ahead to that great Day. So in our next study we will step into God's ultimate answer to all the suffering, pain and death in the world. Prepare to be encouraged as you see that Jesus indeed has overcome the world.

study 6

hope revealed

We now turn the corner in our studies of hope. We have taken a hard look at how God uses the painful challenges of suffering and persecution for His purposes. And as long as life remains on this earth, there will be the need for all of us to endure pain. But if we are to suffer well, we must grasp more clearly the hope that awaits us. And so, in this study we will fast forward to what is to come.

Where we are headed reminds me of driving out of a long, dark tunnel in which the light at the far end has been approaching at an agonizingly slow crawl. Suddenly, everything speeds up as we prepare to burst out of the gloom and fully into the sunlight. All that we have hoped for in Christ is revealed.

At that point in history, the spotlight shifts to fully shine on Jesus. It is all about Him. The God who surely hides Himself (Isaiah 45:15), hides Himself no longer.

Though we do not know when this emergence will precisely occur, we get to watch the "trailer" as God unveils our hope loud and clear through His Word. One day hope will be deferred no more. The heartsickness we have had for our true home in heaven will be a thing of the past, because we will be there. We will eat freely from the tree of life. We shall be fully unearthed. And so, we shall be free forever.

It Is Finished!

>> Before we go back to the future, it will be good to be reminded of what Christ has already done. God, through Christ, has completed all the necessary

groundwork for the realization of our future hope. As Jesus said on the cross, "It is finished!" (John 19:30). Take a look at these powerful Scriptures and then discuss the questions that follow.

But he was pierced for our transgressions, he was crushed for our iniquities; upon him was the chastisement that brought us peace, and with his wounds we are healed. All we like sheep have gone astray; we have turned—every one—to his own way; and the LORD has laid on him the iniquity of us all.
ISAIAH 53:5-6

For our sake he made him to be sin who knew no sin, so that in him we might become the righteousness of God.
2 CORINTHIANS 5:21

Men of Israel, hear these words: Jesus of Nazareth, a man attested to you by God with mighty works and wonders and signs that God did through him in your midst, as you yourselves know – this Jesus, delivered up according to the definite plan and foreknowledge of God, you crucified and killed by the hands of lawless men. God raised him up, loosing the pangs of death, because it was not possible for him to be held by it.
ACTS 2:22-24

Therefore, since the children share in flesh and blood, He Himself likewise also partook of the same, that through death He might render powerless him who had the power of death, that is, the devil, and might free those who through fear of death were subject to slavery all their lives.
HEBREWS 2:14,15 NASB

And if there is no resurrection of the dead, then Christ has not been raised. And if Christ has not been raised, then your faith is useless and you are still guilty of your sins. In that case, all who have died believing in Christ are lost! And if our hope in Christ is only for this life, we are more to be pitied than anyone in the world. But in fact, Christ has been raised from the dead. He is the first of a great harvest of all who have died. So you see, just as death came into the world through a man, now the resurrection from the dead has begun through another man.
1 CORINTHIANS 15:16-21 NLT

Have this mind among yourselves, which is yours in Christ Jesus, who, though he was in the form of God, did not count equality with God a thing to be grasped, but emptied himself, by taking the form of a servant, being born in the likeness of men. And being found in human form, he humbled himself by becoming obedient

to the point of death, even death on a cross. Therefore, God has highly exalted him and bestowed on him the name that is above every name, so that at the name of Jesus every knee should bow, in heaven and on earth and under the earth, and every tongue confess that Jesus Christ is Lord, to the glory of God the Father.
PHILIPPIANS 2:5-11

>> All the Scriptures above pertain to Christ's First Coming as a man, the Messiah, who died on the cross and was raised from the dead. Based on what you have just read, what did Jesus mean when He cried out, "It is finished!"? What exactly did Jesus complete on the cross (and through His resurrection)? Talk about what you think it means that Jesus not only bore our sin but actually "became sin" for us. Why was it impossible for Jesus to be held captive by death? Why is the resurrection of Christ essential for our hope?

As you conclude this first section of this study, spend some time thanking and praising God out loud for His Son, Jesus, and all that He did for us in His First Coming. Encourage individuals to speak up and express their gratitude for the living hope we now have in Christ.

When we think of a conqueror-type animal, a lamb is about as far away from our imaginations as possible. A lion, yes. A tiger, maybe. A bear, perhaps. But never a lamb. No one would ever picture a lamb being able to rescue anything, including itself.

Indeed, it is absolutely impossible, except in the kingdom of God. No one would have ever thought of it. No one but God.

> For in God's realm, humility always conquers pride. Self-sacrificing defeats self-serving. Full surrender annihilates controlling tyranny. Light overcomes darkness. Pure goodness crushes pure evil.

John the Baptist was right when He shouted, *"Behold, the Lamb of God, who takes away the sin of the world!"* (John 1:29).

Dr. Josef Tson was spot on when he wrote, "The strange paradox is that God's method of solving the problem of suffering, of pain, and of death is by suffering and pain and self-sacrifice to the point of death."[23] God's method was a Lamb, Jesus. Nobody saw it coming, especially the devil. It took him totally by surprise.

Satan's fatal flaw was His blinding pride.
His fatal move was having Christ crucified.

Scripture says:

Yet among the mature we do impart wisdom, although it is not a wisdom of this age or of the rulers of this age, who are doomed to pass away. But we impart a secret and hidden wisdom of God, which God decreed before the ages for our glory. None of the rulers of this age understood this, for if they had, they would not have crucified the Lord of glory.

1 CORINTHIANS 2:6-8

Crushing the Serpent's Head

Christ's victory, as Hebrews 2:14,15 declares, spread to conquering the devil, Satan, himself. Unbelievable as it sounds, the Lamb defeated the dragon. The seed of the woman has crushed the serpent's head (Genesis 3:15). God's Word declares:

The person who practices sin belongs to the devil, because the devil has been sinning since the beginning. God's Son appeared for this purpose: to destroy the works of the devil.

1 JOHN 3:8 (CEB)

The works of the devil include all wicked, sinful acts and their consequences, including death. The prophet Isaiah recorded how it all started in Lucifer's heart of defiance when he fell into proud rebellion and sin, becoming our adversary, the devil. Notice also God's judgment of him:

How you are fallen from heaven, O Day Star, son of Dawn! How you are cut down to the ground, you who laid the nations low! You said in your heart, 'I will ascend to heaven; above the stars of God I will set my throne on high; I will sit on the mount of assembly in the far reaches of the north; I will ascend above the heights of the clouds; I will make myself like the Most High.

ISAIAH 14:12-14

When Lucifer vowed five times, "I will...!" that was the first time there was a "will" in the universe other than God's will. Treasonous words! And the words and works of this traitor spread to all mankind throughout history. We too have decreed, "I will...!"

Contrast this self-will with Jesus in the Garden of Gethsemane:

My Father, if it be possible, let this cup pass from me; nevertheless, not as I will, but as you will.

MATTHEW 26:39

Though the battle for our souls was won by Jesus on the cross by His shed blood and death, the battle that Jesus fought Himself was actually won in the Garden of Gethsemane. When Jesus surrendered His will to the Father, the conflict between good and evil was conclusively won in the heart of the Savior. He would go to the cross. Nothing would stop Him.

Rebellion by the prince of darkness could only have been undone by the submitted will of the sun of righteousness (Malachi 4:2). And so, the darkness that came after the sunset was utterly defeated by the "sunrise...from on high" (Luke 1:78).

God has crowned Jesus with glory and honor and has put everything in subjection under his feet (Hebrews 2:7-8a). But, as that passage continues, *"...in putting everything in subjection to him, he left nothing outside his control. At present, we do not yet see everything in subjection to him"* (Hebrews 2:8b).

Indeed, we don't. Not yet. But that day is coming when all will once again be subject to God the Father. Let's take a look at the blazing sunlight at the end of the long, dark tunnel of history.

The Final Victory

>> Below is a sampling of Scriptures that describe Christ's Second Coming... the day that all of those who truly love Him long for (2 Timothy 4:8). After each Scripture are some blank lines. Write in those spaces what each Bible passage teaches about Christ's return and the events thereafter. Do this exercise in advance of your meeting.

When you come together, talk about what you discovered in these passages and then discuss the questions that follow.

But we do not want you to be uninformed, brothers, about those who are asleep, that you may not grieve as others do who have no hope...For the Lord himself will descend from heaven with a cry of command, with the voice of an archangel, and with the sound of the trumpet of God. And the dead in Christ will rise first. Then we who are alive, who are left, will be caught up together with them in the clouds to meet the Lord in the air, and so we will always be with the Lord. Therefore encourage one another with these words.

1 THESSALONIANS 4:13,16-18

Then I saw heaven opened, and behold, a white horse! The one sitting on it is called Faithful and True, and in righteousness he judges and makes war. His eyes are like a flame of fire, and on his head are many diadems, and he has a name written that no one knows but himself. He is clothed in a robe dipped in blood, and the name by which he is called is The Word of God. And the armies of heaven, arrayed in fine linen, white and pure, were following him on white horses. From his mouth comes a sharp sword with which to strike down the nations, and he will rule them with a rod of iron. He will tread the winepress of the fury of the wrath of God the Almighty. On his robe and on his thigh he has a name written, King of kings and Lord of lords.

REVELATION 19:11-16

Then I saw a great white throne and him who was seated on it. From his presence earth and sky fled away, and no place was found for them. And I saw the dead, great and small, standing before the throne, and books were opened. Then another book was opened, which is the book of life. And the dead were judged by what was written in the books, according to what they had done. And the sea gave up the dead who were in it, Death and Hades gave up the dead who were in them, and they were judged, each one of them, according to what they had done. Then Death and Hades were thrown into the lake of fire. This is the second death, the lake of fire. And if anyone's name was not found written in the book of life, he was thrown into the lake of fire.

REVELATION 20:11-15

Then I saw a new heaven and a new earth, for the first heaven and the first earth had passed away, and the sea was no more. And I saw the holy city, new Jerusalem, coming down out of heaven from God, prepared as a bride adorned for her husband. And I heard a loud voice from the throne saying, 'Behold, the dwelling place of God is with man. He will dwell with them, and they will be his people, and God himself will be with them as their God. He will wipe away every tear from their eyes, and death shall be no more, neither shall there be mourning, nor crying, nor pain anymore, for the former things have passed away. And he who was seated on the throne said, 'Behold, I am making all things new.'

REVELATION 21:1-5

>> In the 1 Thessalonians 4 verses above, we are told to encourage one another with these words. In what way(s) are these verses from that chapter meant to encourage us? In Revelation 19, how is Jesus depicted when He comes again (contrasted with His being depicted as a Lamb)? The glimpse these verses from Revelation 20 give of God's judgment of the unbeliever can seem harsh to some. In what way(s), however, can this understanding of God as Judge be a great encouragement to us as we live in a fallen, evil world? What do you find particularly heartening from Revelation 21:1-5?

All Rise!

In our previous study we looked at five attributes of God that are especially helpful in stabilizing us during times of suffering. There is one more that I didn't mention at that time but is highlighted here: God's justice. Justice means more than God punishing evil (though it does involve that).

> God's justice refers to God making everything right, restoring it to the way it is supposed to be.

In our human courts of justice...when things are operating the way they should... the guilty are convicted; the innocent are acquitted; penalties for those culpable are rendered; compensation for the innocent and oppressed are handed down. God's court is like that, only with perfect justice for all. And all this is swept into fulfillment by the Second Coming of the Messiah, the King, who ushers in a whole new realm where righteousness reigns and evil is expunged from the universe. In Christ we will be free forever.

You might find the following acrostic helpful. It is not comprehensive in its treatment of the "end times" but it does hit some of the highlights, focusing on the justice of God:

J— Jesus comes back as the conquering King to set in motion the full and final justice of God

U— Unbelievers who have rejected the King are judged and receive their due punishment forever for high treason

D— Death, the enemy of all that is of God, is vanquished and thrown into the lake of fire forever, where it can never cast its dark shroud of heartless cruelty over the human race ever again. 1 Corinthians 15:54-57 says: "*When the perishable puts on the imperishable, and the mortal puts on immortality, then shall come to pass the saying that is written: 'Death is swallowed up in victory.' 'O death, where is your victory? O death, where is your sting?' The sting of death is sin and the power of sin is the law. But thanks be to God, who gives us the victory through our Lord Jesus Christ.*"

G— God Himself comes to tenderly touch His people and to dwell with them forever and ever.

E— Earth and heaven are destroyed and recreated in righteousness to become our "forever family" home with all of God's saints and angels

>> The following exercise has two options, really three. You can choose either the first topic to discuss in your group or you can choose the second. Or you can do both if you so choose. I think it is important not to rush through this study and these exercises. Scripture says:

Therefore if you have been raised up with Christ, keep seeking the things above, where Christ is, seated at the right hand of God. Set your mind on the things above, not on the things that are on earth. For you have died and your life is hidden with Christ in God. When Christ, who is our life, is revealed, then you also will be revealed with Him in glory.

COLOSSIANS 3:1-4 NASB

>> How often do we do that? How often do we set aside time to think about the world to come and our hope that will one day be unveiled? Not nearly often enough, in my opinion. So here's our chance to camp out in eternity for a little while. A deep drink from these waters renews our hope and grants us grace and strength for the battles that remain here on the earth.

<u>Option One:</u> One of the things that touches people about Revelation 21 is that God Himself will wipe away the tears from our eyes. This indicates that in heaven, at least at first, there is the memory of our suffering. God doesn't ignore the pain we have been through here on earth. And rather than just magically removing all painful memories before we get to heaven, He waits until we get there, then addresses each experience of pain, taking time with each saint personally to bring His tender touch and comfort. Scripture says:

You keep track of all my sorrows. You have collected all my tears in your bottle. You have recorded each one in your book.

PSALM 56:8 (NLT)

>> I believe that it is for this moment in eternity that God has kept our tears. As He wipes them away, He ushers us into a healing place where there will be no more crying or sorrow or death or pain.

Talk about the hurts or times of mourning in your life for which you are so looking forward to Jesus personally touching you and wiping away your tears. It is important that everyone be respectful of those having the courage to share. Though full healing will take place in heaven (Revelation 22:1,2), our gracious and merciful God might use this time to touch His saints even before we get there.

<u>Option Two:</u> Since almost the beginning of time, the devil has caused havoc, mayhem, pandemonium, death and destruction. Sorry, Keith Richards and Mick Jagger, there's no sympathy for the devil. He gave none; he deserves none; he gets none. Scripture says:

And when the thousand years are ended, Satan will be released from his prison and will come out to deceive the nations that are at the four corners of the earth, Gog and Magog, to gather them to battle, their number is like the sand of the sea. And they marched up over the broad plain of the earth and surrounded the camp of the saints and the beloved city, but fire came down from heaven and consumed them, and the devil who had deceived them was thrown into the lake of fire and sulfur where the beast and the false prophet were, and they will be tormented day and night forever and ever.

REVELATION 20:7-10

>> When you read those words (and make sure you read them out loud in your group), there ought to be something within you that leaps for joy. This is right. This is just. This is as it should be. This is necessary for God to secure His kingdom and rule in righteousness forever. Maybe, like me, you wouldn't mind it at all if God let you have a hand in this matter!

In your group, encourage each person to think about a time in their life or in the lives of those they love in which the devil got his way...in harming or even ruining those lives. Talk about those incidents and how it makes you feel to know that one day Satan will get what he has always deserved. God will avenge every evil deed Satan has ever perpetrated.

We are not expected to forgive the devil. On the contrary, we wait eagerly yet patiently for his destruction. That is the only thing that will make this right. May you find comfort in this reminder of the justice of God. It is part of our hope.

In the meantime, we do everything we can by the power of God's Spirit to win the lost and set captives free. Scripture calls it binding the "strong man" and plundering his house (Mark 3:26-28). Let's do this!

One More Gaze Upward

As we wrap up this study on our revealed hope, I want to briefly take one more look at "the things above" before life forces us to come back down to earth and conclude. Consider this:

What will it be like to have only the purest thoughts, motives, words and actions? When absolutely nothing we think, feel, say or do will ever be tainted by sin again? Where all the infirmities of our flesh are no more. No more migraines, kidney stones, bouts of depression, seasons of anxiety, fits of rage, addictions, cancer, heart disease, strokes, conflicts with God, battles with people, encounters with a hostile world of nature, or spiritual battles. Just peace.

We will be finally and fully *unearthed*. We will be finally and fully free...forever. I can only imagine.

What exactly we will become in heaven is still a mystery; we do not know fully. But we do know some things. We will be even greater than the angels (Psalm 8:5) and, in fact, will judge them (1 Corinthians 6:3). That's pretty mind-blowing, considering how awesome angels are.

Even more amazing is that we will be like Jesus Himself...not Divine, but fully Christ-like in character.

The Bible tells us:

See what great love the Father has lavished on us, that we should be called children of God! And that is what we are! The reason the world does not know us is that it did not know him. Dear friends, now we are children of God, and what we will be has not yet been made known. But we know that when Christ appears, we shall be like him, for we shall see him as he is. All who have this hope in him purify themselves, just as he is pure.

1 JOHN 3:1-3 (NIV)

So how shall we now live?...As deeply loved children of God, who want to accelerate the work of God making us pure by purifying ourselves. Now. Today.

Jesus said, "Blessed are the pure in heart for they shall see God" (Matthew 5:8). May that be a deep and lasting yearning of our souls...to see God, both through a glass darkly now, but then face to face (1 Corinthians 13:12). To look into the face of God will be the best of the best, the joy of all joys, the fulfillment of every righteous heart. And yet, there is more...

Now the Lord is the Spirit, and where the Spirit of the Lord is, there is freedom. And we all, with unveiled face, beholding the glory of the Lord, are being transformed into the same image from one degree of glory to another. For this comes from the Lord who is the Spirit.

2 CORINTHIANS 3:17-18

Glory? For you and me? As incredible as that seems, it sure sounds like it. That will be the subject of *Study Seven*.

study 7

glory, honor & peace

Jesus had just finished speaking with a wealthy young man who rejected His invitation to sell his possessions, give to the poor and come follow Him. Jesus then put a cap on that part of the conversation by commenting on how hard it is for people with lots of money to come into God's kingdom.

That statement astonished the disciples (who must have thought the wealthy would be the first to make it!).

"Who then can be saved?" the forlorn disciples asked (Matthew 19:25).

Jesus, never missing a chance to broaden a conversation to include everyone said, *"With man this is impossible, but with God all things are possible"* (Matthew 19:26).

Coming from our strong, new covenant background of understanding "salvation by grace alone through faith alone in Jesus alone," had we been standing there we would have been vigorously nodding our heads. Theology 101.

Peter then spoke up. Nothing unusual there! But he was likely mouthing what all the rest of Jesus' followers were thinking:

See, we have left everything and followed you. What then will we have?
MATTHEW 19:27

It is important to note what Jesus didn't do and say. He *didn't* whirl around with righteous indignation and rebuke Peter, saying:

"Why you ungrateful, greedy sinner! I have already given you this incredibly important place as one of My disciples, and now you want more? You ought to be ashamed of yourself. Go have a Quiet Time and come back when you have repented of your self-centered ways!"

Rewards and Risks

Jesus, instead, was very clear:

Truly, I say to you, in the new world, when the Son of Man will sit on his glorious throne, you who have followed me will also sit on twelve thrones, judging the twelve tribes of Israel. And everyone who has left houses or brothers or sisters or father or mother or children or lands, for my name's sake, will receive a hundredfold and will inherit eternal life. But many who are first will be last, and the last first.

MATTHEW 19:28-30

>> Jesus wanted His disciples to know what reward was coming down the road for them as they were being trained for a lifetime of (often very difficult) ministry. It is obvious our Lord thought that the anticipation of future rewards was a valid motivation for present day service.

In your discussion groups talk about these questions: We can certainly see the validity of Jesus' disciples getting eternal rewards, but will there be anything for the rest of us? Should there be? Is it a valid motivation for everyday believers to anticipate heavenly rewards? Why or why not? Wouldn't looking forward to rewards in heaven tend to make us like "spiritual mercenaries," only doing the work because one day we will get "paid"? What do you think?

There have been Protestant theologians over the centuries that have not wanted to touch the doctrine of eternal rewards with a ten-foot-pole. They were nervous that it could lead to a belief that our good works merited rewards from God and that He would be obligated to "pay" us for those works, running contrary to the doctrine of grace.

Others might be concerned that any mention of glory for God's people would by default distract from God's glory. It could be seen as threatening "Soli Deo gloria"—Glory to God alone.

Despite potential risks involved with giving out heavenly rewards to His children, God not only gives them, but lets us know in advance they are coming. Of that the Bible is clear. This is totally consistent with His pattern of generosity throughout history.

For example, God knew many would misunderstand and even twist Scripture for evil purposes, yet He gave us the Bible anyway. He also knew that spiritual gifts could be misused, ignored and bring division to the body of Christ, yet He gave us spiritual gifts anyway. In fact, if you think about it, every good gift from the Father's hand has somehow been misused or abused by the human race, and yet God gave us good gifts anyway. He is a generous God. It is His nature.

Rewards and Awards

So what awaits the child of God when he or she gets to heaven? What does the Bible teach?

>> In advance of your discussion, read over the following Scriptures and write in the blanks following what those verses say about heavenly rewards. Then discuss what you came up with when you meet in your group.

There will be tribulation and distress for every human being who does evil, the Jew first and also the Greek, but glory and honor and peace for everyone who does good, the Jew first and also the Greek.
ROMANS 2:9-10

To them God chose to make known how great among the Gentiles are the riches of the glory of this mystery, which is Christ in you, the hope of glory.
COLOSSIANS 1:27

For those whom he foreknew he also predestined to be conformed to the image of his Son in order that he might be the firstborn among many brothers. And those whom he predestined he also called, and those whom he called he also justified, and those whom he justified he also glorified.
ROMANS 8:29-30

Henceforth there is laid up for me the crown of righteousness, which the Lord, the righteous judge, will award to me on that Day, and not only to me but also to all who have loved his appearing.
2 TIMOTHY 4:8

So let no one boast in men. For all things are yours, whether Paul or Apollos or Cephas or the world or life or death or the present or the future—all are yours, and you are Christ's, and Christ is God's.
1 CORINTHIANS 3:21-21

The Spirit bears witness with our spirit that we are children of God, and if children, then heirs—heirs of God and fellow heirs with Christ, provided we suffer with him in order that we may also be glorified with him.
ROMANS 8:16-17

Blessed are the poor in spirit, for theirs is the kingdom of heaven.
MATTHEW 5:3

Blessed are the meek, for they shall inherit the earth.
MATTHEW 5:5

Glory, honor, peace and much more. Those are the things that await us.

Peace? We are comfortable with that reality though we should never forget its power. Because of our faith, God declares us "not guilty" and we have peace with God through our Lord Jesus Christ when formerly we were His enemies (Romans 5:1-10). That's a really big deal. But we tend to be okay with thinking about God granting us peace with Himself.

Honor? Okay. We can maybe wrap our minds around that one too, though it is pretty amazing.

Jesus said, *"If anyone serves me, he must follow me; and where I am, there will my servant be also. If anyone serves me, the Father will honor him"* (John 12:26).

Though a servant's faithfulness is his duty, Jesus promised to honor those who serve Him.

But glory? That is almost beyond belief. Just stagger over to the mirror early tomorrow morning, rub the crust out of your eyes, and take a good look at what you see. Glory? I don't think so. At least not to your human eyes. But what does God see? He sees one of His children who has already been glorified, though that glory is obviously now veiled.

One day in heaven it will no longer be hidden, as Colossians 3:4 says, *"When Christ who is your life appears, then you also will appear with him in glory."*

Hard to believe, but true.

What exactly is "glory"? It's kind of difficult to define, though when we see it, we'll know it.

> Glory is radiance, the brilliant, outward display of perfection and holiness.

If you look carefully you can see a glimmer of it on the faces and in the eyes of mature, godly, loving saints. Just wait until heaven.

Should we be concerned that God's radiant glory shining in us and through us will somehow distract from or diminish Christ's glory? Of course not. Why should it? How could it? In fact, the glory of His grace is magnified, since He freely and generously shares it with us.

Now, you might protest that God said in Isaiah 42:8 (NASB), *"I am the LORD, that is My name! I will not give my glory to another, nor My praise to graven images."* Clearly the meaning in that passage is that no other god or idol will ever receive any of the glory of God.

But we are not idols. We are not God's rivals. We are His body, His family, God's children. And is it not God's prerogative to glorify Christ as Head and the Church as His body? After all, we are in Christ and He is in us.

It is enough reward to think about our receiving glory, honor and peace, but there is more. In heaven, we will also receive a crown, the crown of righteousness.

Scripture doesn't explain what the crown of righteousness is, but I tend to think it is a literal, visible, tangible crown. That makes sense based on Revelation 4:10.

There it describes the 24 elders laying or casting down their crowns before God Himself. It is hard to lay down something that one cannot hold. See also 1 Peter 5:4 where all elders who serve the Lord Jesus well will receive "the unfading crown of glory."

So, there will be glory, honor, peace and a crown. But that is not all!

God's Word also says that those who are poor in spirit and meek (humble) will inherit the kingdom of heaven and the earth as well. I believe that is referring to the new heavens and earth, because the days are numbered for the present ones. Peter wrote:

But the day of the Lord will come like a thief, and then the heavens will pass away with a roar, and the heavenly bodies will be burned up and dissolved, and the earth and the works that are done on it will be exposed. Since all these things are thus to be dissolved, what sort of people ought you to be in lives of holiness and godliness, waiting for and hastening the coming of the day of God, because of which the heavens will be set on fire and dissolved, and the heavenly bodies will melt as they burn! But according to his promise we are waiting for new heavens and a new earth in which righteousness dwells.

2 PETER 3:10-13

The re-creation of the heavens and earth in which righteousness (and righteous people!) will dwell is an invitation for the imagination to go wild. Since we will be like Jesus (1 John 3:3), we will be able to do what Jesus did in His resurrected body. He could eat or not eat. He could pass through walls. He could appear and reappear. I believe it is not a stretch to say, "So will we!"

It's like all the dreams we have ever had of superpowers will become a reality.

Can you imagine being able to travel at the speed of thought? To explore the vast reaches of the universe and have the brain capacity to take it all in? Or just hang out, doing incredibly important kingdom work for Jesus here on Earth?

The adventure of all this will dwarf anything we can currently experience, and no doubt far transcend anything that we can dream of now.

> We could say that once the old earth is gone and we are totally "unearthed," we will become re-earthed on the new Earth!

What no eye has seen, nor ear heard, nor the heart of man imagined, what God has prepared for those who love him.

1 CORINTHIANS 2:9

And as if all this were not enough, Paul in his exuberant extolling of God's virtue of goodness wrote that "all things" are ours in Christ (1 Corinthians 3:21).

What in the world (or out of this world) can that mean? I don't think any of us can begin to fathom the vastness of such generosity.

Do we deserve these kinds of rewards? Absolutely not. They are free gifts of God's grace, but they all come by virtue of our being born again into the family of God and becoming His children, God's heirs (John 1:12; Romans 8:16). It is the inheritance that Peter wrote about in his first letter, an inheritance that provides joy in the midst of the distress caused by trials and testing now:

Blessed be the God and Father of our Lord Jesus Christ! According to his great mercy, he has caused us to be born again to a living hope through the resurrection of Jesus Christ from the dead, to an inheritance that is imperishable, undefiled, and unfading, kept in heaven for you, who by God's power are being guarded through faith for a salvation ready to be revealed in the last time. In this you rejoice, though now for a little while, if necessary, you have been grieved by various trials, so that the tested genuineness of your faith—more precious than gold that perishes though it is tested by fire—may be found to result in praise and glory and honor at the revelation of Jesus Christ.

1 PETER 1:3-7

>> It seems very appropriate at this point to pause to worship God. Just like Peter gave praise and honor to God (*"Blessed be the God and Father..."*), so should we. Take some time in your groups to thank and praise God out loud for His generosity in providing such gifts to us and so marvelous an inheritance to His children. Then ask the Lord for the ability to rejoice in what securely awaits in heaven, no matter what trials and testing our faith might be undergoing right now.

Are All Rewards Created Equal?

>> Have some members in your group read the following scenarios out loud and then discuss the questions that follow:

There are two genuine believers in Jesus living in a nation in which it is illegal to convert to Christianity. One of the believers keeps quiet about her new faith. She doesn't tell her family though she does go into chat rooms online and, under an alias, tells of her faith. She reads her Bible and is growing in the Lord, but she lives her faith under the radar and is able to go about life pretty much as she always has done. The other believer connects with the underground Church, meeting with other believers, despite the risk. She begins to share the gospel with family and friends and her family turns her in to the government police. She is convicted of the crimes of converting to the Christian faith and seeking to convert others. She is imprisoned, enduring numerous beatings, as the authorities try to extract information about other believers from her. They are not successful in breaking her.

There are two genuine believers in Jesus living in America. One of the believers is a faithful church member and attendee, serving in his local fellowship. He is a solid citizen and a hardworking, trustworthy employee. He and his wife live in a neighborhood in which they are respected for being good people and keeping a nice lawn. They prefer to let their lives be their witness and do not want to offend or alienate anyone by being too outspoken. The other believer is growing in his faith, is part of a community of believers and is also a faithful witness at work. He can be a bit brash and abrasive and some of his extended family roll their eyes when he inevitably talks about Jesus at holidays and family reunions. He has lost some friends on his street and on the job for his "fanatical" beliefs, but has also seen some of his neighbors and fellow employees come to faith in Jesus.

These two scenarios are actually very similar. The only difference is the cultural context in which they take place. One environment is spiritually hostile and dangerous; the other context is far less so.

Here are the questions to discuss: Do you think both believers in each scenario

ought to receive the same rewards in heaven? Why or why not?

We have already seen and discussed the amazing grace of Jesus in granting all His true followers astronomically generous rewards in heaven. Just the joy of seeing Jesus face to face will be incredible. Add to that an eternity free from all sin with a new, glorified resurrected body like Jesus' and our imaginations are already stretched to the limit. If that weren't plenty, include our inheritance as heirs of God and joint heirs with Christ which includes the new heavens and earth, and you have an absolutely breathtaking reward.

Who could ask for or even expect more? None of us. We are already overwhelmed. Our mouths are shut. We wouldn't dare say, "Umm Jesus, that doesn't seem like enough..."

>> The Scriptures that we have already looked at, however, do not exhaust the supply of verses about rewards in heaven. There are more. Have some members of your group read the following Bible passages out loud and then discuss the questions that follow. Look up the Scriptures ahead of time and use the blanks following to write down any thoughts or questions you have

Blessed are those who are persecuted for righteousness' sake, for theirs is the kingdom of heaven.
MATTHEW 5:10

Blessed are you when others revile you and persecute you and utter all kinds of evil against you falsely on my account. Rejoice and be glad, for your reward is great in heaven, for so they persecuted the prophets who were before you.
MATTHEW 5:11-12

Do not fear what you are about to suffer. Behold, the devil is about to throw some of you into prison, that you may be tested, and for ten days you will have tribulation. Be faithful unto death, and I will give you the crown of life.
REVELATION 2:10-11

For we who live are always being given over to death for Jesus' sake, so that the life of Jesus also may be manifested in our mortal flesh. So death is at work in us, but life in you...So we do not lose heart. Though our outer self is wasting away, our inner self is being renewed day by day. For this light momentary affliction is preparing for us an eternal weight of glory beyond all comparison, as we look not to the things that are seen but to the things that are unseen. For the things that are seen are transient, but the things that are unseen are eternal.
2 CORINTHIANS 4:11-12,16-18

The Spirit himself bears witness with our spirit that we are children of God, and if children, then heirs—heirs of God and fellow heirs with Christ, provided we suffer with him in order that we may also be glorified with him. For I consider that the sufferings of this present time are not worth comparing with the glory that is to be revealed to us.

ROMANS 8:16-18

Blessed is the man who remains steadfast under trial, for when he has stood the test he will receive the crown of life, which God has promised to those who love him.

JAMES 1:12

>> Questions: Aside from being followers of Christ, what do all the people these Scriptures refer to have in common? According to these verses, what are the rewards to those who suffer and stand firm in Christ in the midst of trial and persecution? Based on the Scriptures above, do there seem to be greater rewards in heaven for those who undergo suffering, persecution and even martyrdom for Christ than for those who don't? Does that seem right to you? Explain your answer.

We all go through trials and suffering in our lives. Some of it is just because we live in a fallen world and things go wrong. It's not the direct result of our sin; it is just life on a corrupted planet. Stuff breaks. Accidents happen. Work is hard. Our bodies get injured or sick. We die.

Some of our suffering is because of sins we have committed or wrong life choices we have made. We smoke, drink, or eat too much and suffer the physical consequences. We work too long and hard, get stressed out, have high blood pressure, and maybe even alienate our spouse and kids. There doesn't seem to be any particular glory for enduring such things.

Scripture, however, seems to give special commendation to those who are afflicted for the cause of Christ and who stand firm in righteousness when tempted to give up. And particular attention seems to be given to those who lose their lives for the sake of Christ. A brief, but touching account in Revelation 6:9-11 gives us an example of that special treatment:

When he opened the fifth seal, I saw under the altar the souls of those who had been slain for the word of God and for the witness they had borne. They cried out with a loud voice, 'O Sovereign Lord, holy and true, how long before you will judge and avenge our blood on those who dwell on the earth?' Then they were each given a white robe and told to rest a little longer, until the number of their fellow servants and their brothers should be complete, who were to be killed as they themselves had been.

REVELATION 6:9-11

I don't know about you, but this all seems very just and right to me. For those dear saints that have endured grueling punishment and cruel beatings for the cause of Christ, even to the point of death, it makes complete sense that God would reward them in some greater measure. But my opinion means nothing; Scripture means everything, and the Bible indicates this is indeed what will happen. And the assurance and reassurance of this future hope to those suffering greatly for the cause of Christ grants inestimable joy and strength for them to endure today.

> Something very important should be noted at this juncture: There will be no envy in heaven. There will be no competition or comparison. There will be no resentment.

When we are all standing before the Lord and witness those who were persecuted and even martyred for their faith receiving greater rewards than us, we will all be cheering. We will worship God for His great grace and rejoice in the special glory given to those precious saints. We will probably all go forward to congratulate those glorified martyrs for their steadfastness in trial. And we'll want to hear their stories to the glory of God.

Rewards for Faithfulness

It is hard to know what all our heavenly rewards will actually be like, since we only have an earthly frame of reference from which to operate. One day we will know fully; we only see a glimpse now. But Jesus' parable of the talents gives us a hint.

>> You likely recall the story Jesus told. A wealthy man was headed out of town for a while and while he was gone, he gave three of his employees a job to do. They were each given a certain amount of money to invest. One was given five talents, another two and still another one. Although scholars differ on the modern-day monetary equivalent of a talent (depending on whether the talent was of silver or gold), suffice it to say that a talent was a lot of money. The one given five talents invested wisely and earned five more. Likewise, the one given two earned two more. The third man who was given one talent buried it and earned no interest, much to the great displeasure of the wealthy man when he returned. You can read the whole story in Matthew 25:14-30.

What I want to focus on were the (identical) statements spoken to the two faithful employees. The wealthy employer said to both, *"Well done, good and faithful servant. You have been faithful over a little; I will set you over much. Enter into the joy of your master"* (Matthew 25:21,23).

Here are the questions to discuss: Were the amounts initially entrusted to the two faithful servants identical? On what basis do you think the amounts entrusted to these two were determined? Later on, the one talent that had been given to the unfaithful servant was given to the one who now had ten. Why do you think the wealthy employer did that? When the employer (master) told the two "I will set you over much," what do you think Jesus was talking about?

The judgment on the one unfaithful employee or servant (being cast into outer darkness where there will be weeping and gnashing of teeth, see v. 30), was clearly a final judgment in eternity as opposed to some earthly punishment. Therefore, we can surmise that the rewards for the two faithful employees were also heavenly or eternal rewards as well.

Did you catch what the reward was? Being put in charge of much. Where? Clearly, this would have to be in the new creation when the new heavens and earth are created. This parallels other Scriptures where saints are promised the responsibility of judging the world (1 Corinthians 6:2) and judging angels (1 Corinthians 6:3). Remember, too, that Jesus had promised His disciples that they would sit on thrones (Matthew 19:27,28). Sitting on thrones indicates judging and ruling.

Though the specifics have yet to be revealed, it is also clear that those who are faithful servants of the Lord Jesus on the earth will be involved in judgment and rulership in the new creation.

One thing that strikes me as encouraging is that there will be work for us to do in heaven and that work will bring joy. Right now, you might have a hard time putting the words "work" and "joy" in the same sentence, but one Day you will.

Despite some cultural caricatures, we will not spend eternity lounging on pillowy clouds strumming harps. Thank God! The holy, joyful, fulfilling work that Adam and Eve had in the Garden of Eden before they messed everything up, will be restored (and magnified!) in the kingdom of God. And it is very possible that those whose characters have deepened and matured in godliness, humility and sacrifice on earth will be granted, as a reward of their faithfulness, more leadership responsibility in the kingdom of God. That is what the Scriptures seem to be saying.

The Judgment of Believers

So how does the distribution of rewards unfold? Where and when does that happen? This passage from God's Word tells us:

So we are always of good courage. We know that while we are at home in the body we are away from the Lord, for we walk by faith, not by sight. Yes, we are of good courage, and we would rather be away from the body and at home with the Lord. So whether we are at home or away, we make it our aim to please him. For we must all appear before the judgment seat of Christ, so that each one may receive what is due for what he has done in the body, whether good or evil.

2 CORINTHIANS 5:6-10

For the believer, there is no judgment for sin. Christ took on Himself all God's righteous indignation for our wickedness and paid the punishment of death on our behalf.

God is not going to say to His children at the judgment, "Well, I do have a few bones to pick with you regarding some of your worst sins." That will never happen. Our sins and lawless deeds He will remember no more (Hebrews 10:17).

Paul said his aim or ambition was to please God. What a role model for us! He urged us to "try and discern what is pleasing to the Lord" (Ephesians 5:10). Why? Because there will be another judgment for believers, at which time God's rewards will be handed out.

>> It is a sobering thing to realize that one day we will all appear before the judgment seat of Christ. No exceptions. Paul said, even though he knew this judgment was forthcoming, he was always of good courage. He was not afraid to stand before Christ. Should we be?

Read the following Scripture out loud in your group and then discuss the questions that follow.

According to the grace of God given to me, like a skilled master builder I laid a foundation, and someone else is building upon it. Let each one take care how he builds upon it. For no one can lay a foundation other than that which is laid, which is Jesus Christ. Now if anyone builds on the foundation with gold, silver, precious stones, wood, hay, straw—each one's work will become manifest, for the Day will disclose it, because it will be revealed by fire, and the fire will test what sort of work each one has done. If the work that anyone has built on the foundation survives, he will receive a reward. If anyone's work is burned up, he will suffer loss, though he himself will be saved, but only as through fire.

1 CORINTHIANS 3:10-15

>> Questions: This passage of Scripture is clearly not talking about a judgment to determine whether a person has eternal life or not; it is a judgment of something else. What will be judged on this Day? How will our works be judged? What will happen to the works described as "gold, silver, precious stones"? What will happen to those works determined to be "wood, hay,

straw"? What do you think distinguishes one group of works from the other in the eyes of God? What does the one whose works are "gold, silver, precious stones" receive from God? What happens with the one whose works are judged as "wood, hay, straw"?

One thing is very clear from this Scripture:

It will matter in eternity how we live our lives now.

I don't know about you, but I am not excited about the prospect of watching much or all of my life's work become a heavenly bonfire. Paul urges us to "take care" how we build. That is, all our good works must start out with the foundation of Jesus. He has to be in charge of what we do. He must be the One empowering us to do it. He is the One to receive the honor.

And when we seek to help people in that Name, the works will be good (as beautiful and precious as gold, silver and precious gems); the works will survive the judgment; and we will be rewarded. If not, the judgment will show their worthlessness and they will be destroyed forever. That will not be easy to take. We will suffer loss, but Jesus is tender and merciful and, as we have seen, He will wipe away every tear (Revelation 21:4). Though our works may be burned to ashes, we will still be saved.

This is sort of a "bad news, good news" scenario. The bad news is that every work we do as a follower of Christ will be remembered and judged. Much of what we perhaps thought were great things we did for Christ may not end up surviving the judgment after all. The good news is that everything we do as a follower of Christ will be remembered and judged. Much of what we deemed insignificant and trivial will glow with glory and come forth as gold, silver and precious stones. In this case, beauty IS in the eye of the Beholder, and the Beholder is Christ.

Jesus said, *"And if anyone gives even a cup of cold water to one of these little ones who is my disciple, truly I tell you, that person will certainly not lose their reward"* (Matthew 10:42 NIV).

That's comforting. We can all do that and much more.

Again, *it will matter in eternity how we live our lives now.*

So how shall we live now? That is the subject of our eighth and final study.

study 8

what now?

We are now approaching the end of the road. I trust these studies have proven to be a worthwhile journey for you. Perhaps you are sensing that something fundamentally has changed in your way of looking at life, death, suffering, hope and eternity. My hope and prayer are that your freedom and joy and capacity to enjoy life and endure hardship this side of heaven have increased. If so, to God be the glory!

But before we wrap things up and hit the finish line, we still have one more very important step to take.

In this eighth and final study, together we want to take a stab at answering the apostle Peter's question in his second letter:

> *Since all these things [present heavens and earth] are thus to be dissolved,* ***what sort of people ought you to be in lives of holiness and godliness?***
>
> 2 PETER 3:11 (EMPHASIS MINE)

Basically, Peter was saying, "Um, you do realize that nothing you see around you (aside from people) is going to last much longer. In fact, it is all going up in smoke one day. So how might that reality change the way you look at things and live your life now?"

Our brother, Peter, asks a very crucial question. It would be wise to ask God what He thinks.

>> Take a minute to pause before beginning this final study to inquire of God, praying the following prayer out loud together in your group:

PRAY

Dear Father, You are an amazing God, Your Son is a wonderful Savior, and Your Spirit is such a powerful and faithful Comforter. Thank You that You are here with us as we meet together and that one Day we will see You face to face. We will be free forever, serving with You in the new heavens and earth. I can't wait. I know that what I do during my stay here matters in eternity. I am sorry for the ways You know that I have not lived my life on earth with eternity in mind. Thank You for Your gracious forgiveness. Now that my heart and mind are growing in their capacity to focus on things above, would You please show me how to live my life now in light of eternity. Our hope is in You alone. Amen.

You may have heard the old expression, "He is so heavenly-minded, he is no earthly good." That is not in the Bible, by the way. And I cannot imagine the apostle Paul grunting in agreement with that statement. The idea, I suppose, was that if someone were overly religious and fanatical about their faith, they would somehow lose touch with reality here on earth.

To be perfectly honest, I am much more concerned that too many followers of Christ, especially in affluent cultures, are "so earthly-minded, they are no heavenly good." Strong words, I know, but I am serious.

Maybe I can sum up what I am seeking to accomplish in this book and in this study by saying, "Let's become *more* heavenly-minded so that we can become *more* earthly good!" Agreed?

Okay. Let's continue.

Partnership with God

In answering Peter's question in 2 Peter 3:11, the first thing we need to dig our teeth into is grace. God is not looking for some kind of Christian behavior modification here. God forbid that I conclude this book by jumping into some "Do this, don't do that" advice that stinks of legalism and self-effort. That would be doomed to failure from the start anyway.

>> In advance of your group meeting, take a look at the following Scriptures. In the blanks provided after each Bible passage, write down what those verses teach about where our capacity to change, obey and grow come from.

Once you get together with your group, discuss the questions that follow these Scriptures.

I am the vine, you are the branches. Whoever abides in me and I in him, he it is that bears much fruit, for apart from me you can do nothing.

JESUS'S WORDS – JOHN 15:5

Therefore, my beloved, as you have always obeyed, so now, not only as in my presence but much more in my absence, work out your own salvation with fear and trembling, for it is God who works in you, both to will and to work for his good pleasure.

PHILIPPIANS 2:12-13

Him [Christ] we proclaim, warning everyone and teaching everyone with all wisdom, that we may present everyone mature in Christ. For this I toil, struggling with all his energy that he powerfully works within me.

COLOSSIANS 1:28-29

But by the grace of God, I am what I am, and his grace toward me was not in vain. On the contrary, I worked harder than any of them, though it was not I, but the grace of God that is with me.

1 CORINTHIANS 15:10

Rather train yourself for godliness, for while bodily training is of some value, godliness is of value in every way, as it holds promise for the present life and also for the life to come.

1 TIMOTHY 4:7B-8

>> Questions: What can we learn from Jesus' description of Himself as the vine and we as branches? What role does the vine play? What role does the branch play? What do you think it means to "work out your own salvation"? According to these verses above, is working hard for Christ wrong? Why or why not? What does Paul tell Timothy is more valuable than physical fitness?

In what way does godliness hold promise for "the present life"? In what way does it hold promise for "the life to come"? How do you think you can train yourself for the purpose of godliness now?

Nothing of eternal value gets done if we go it alone. But nothing gets done through us either if we simply go passive and think it is all up to God. Kingdom work is a partnership between God and us. God gives us the desire and power to do His will (Philippians 2:12,13) as we remain close to and dependent on Jesus (John 15:5). We are then energized to work hard in what He has called us to do, finding as we move forward that it is God's mighty power and grace that is working with us and through us.

It is clear, however, that the onus of responsibility to live our lives in Christ and to grow in godliness is on us. Christ is the "constant"; we are the "variable." God is always available to strengthen us with the awesome power that raised Christ from the dead (Ephesians 1:19-21). His grace works in us and through us (1 Corinthians 15:10). The question is: Will we "buy into" God's work, cooperating with His plan and purpose? That's called obedience.

As Paul taught Timothy, we need to discipline ourselves for the purpose of becoming godly. It is a training that involves practice and perseverance. And it requires sacrifice, just like an athlete.

No, God is not necessarily telling you to cancel your fitness club membership. But His expectation is that we would "work out" more diligently for our spiritual growth and health than we do to try and achieve six-pack abs.

What do we need to do (or not do) to get into better spiritual shape? Paul wrote:

Do you not know that in a race all the runners run, but only one receives the prize? So run that you may obtain it. Every athlete exercises self-control in all things. They do it to receive a perishable wreath, but we an imperishable. So I do not run aimlessly; I do not box as one beating the air. But I discipline my body and keep it under control, lest after preaching to others I myself should be disqualified.

1 CORINTHIANS 9:24-27

Paul's words are sobering. Even he faced the possibility of being knocked out of the race. This was not a question of his salvation, but a matter of his being fit for kingdom ministry. Though his teaching on spiritual warfare makes it clear he was not ignorant of the devil's schemes (2 Corinthians 2:11), he realized the greatest threat to his continued usefulness to God were his own fleshly desires. So it is with us.

Holiness and Godliness

>> This next exercise is where the rubber meets the road.

Good teaching can become just "mind candy" unless it involves obedience. When we obey what God is telling us to do, then real heart change and life transformation can take place.

Each of us is urged in Scripture to be a "doer of the Word" and not merely a "hearer who deceives himself" (see James 1:22). We want to assist you in doing that.

According to Peter's question in 2 Peter 3:11, the two character qualities we are to develop are "holiness" and "godliness." They are related but not the same. Holiness involves our being set apart from the world to God, and godliness refers to our becoming more and more like Jesus.

As always, I encourage you to work on this assignment on your own, ahead of time. Then come prepared to share with your group what the Lord showed you. First, please join me in prayer:

PRAY

Dear Father, You inspired Peter to urge us to become people growing in holiness and godliness, in light of the transience of this present universe. It takes humility to admit my need to grow and courage to obey You in whatever You show me. By Your Spirit I fully surrender to Your good, acceptable and perfect will (Romans 12:2). Please open my heart to what You are saying to me now, that I might choose to trust You to change me and make me more like Your Son. I know I can't change on my own. I totally need Your power and grace. Amen.

>> You have just asked the Lord for His guidance; you can trust He will answer.

In light of the call to "holiness," being set apart from this world system to God, complete the following statements (based on what you sense the Lord saying to you):

I can really do without ______________________________

I need to cut back on ______________________________

I would be better off if I didn't ______________________________

>> You have just asked the Lord for His guidance; you can trust He will answer.

In light of the call to "godliness," becoming more like the Lord Jesus, complete the following statements (based on what you sense the Lord saying to you):

I need God's grace to enable me to ______________________________

____

My personal walk with God would grow if I ______________________________

____

One way I can better love the people around me is by ______________________________

____

>> Now, go back and put a check mark by one or two statements in each category that you believe to be the most important for you right now.

An example might be: I will cut back 45 minutes of gaming time each night and instead spend that time reading God's Word and praying (or leading the family in devotions).

Or: I will give up watching Netflix on Tuesdays this month to attend the evening class at church on how to share my faith in Jesus.

It's really pretty simple and straightforward. Just make sure the choices you make will bring substantive change as you obey what the Lord has shown you to do. Don't just come up with something dumb like "I will abstain from liver and onions and Brussels sprouts for Jesus."

Discuss in your group what the Lord showed you and pray for one another that He would grant His grace for obedience and for real life change to take place. This is all part of the process of becoming "unearthed."

Did you sense the Lord guiding you into what His priorities are for you right now? The reason I had you select only one or two things from each category is that trying to do too much too fast can be overwhelming. You can always tackle other areas later. The joy and satisfaction you get from seeing God work in one or two areas of your life will encourage you to keep going!

Having said that, it is possible you are seeing the need in your life for a deeper spiritual "house cleaning," involving multiple areas. That's totally okay. If that is the case, I strongly encourage you to go through *The Steps to Freedom in Christ*. Better yet, have someone trained in using that ministry tool take you through the "Steps." You can purchase copies of *The Steps to Freedom in Christ* online at www.freedominchrist.com .

Don't worry if you felt a bit of tension going through the exercise above. That is normal. Any time we bump up against the need for change in our lives, there will be internal conflict. Count on it. Change is hard, but growing in holiness and godliness requires change...good change...and God will guide you and strengthen you all the way through that process of transformation. In Christ, you can do this!

In the Conclusion to this book, you will read some of my thoughts as to where things are headed in the days to come. One thing clear from Scripture is that things will get pretty dicey prior to the Second Coming of our Lord Jesus. What more can we do to get ready?

Turning an attentive ear and obedient heart to God and His Word as we grow in holiness and godliness in the context of a vibrant, community of Spirit-filled believers is crucial. So is being active in spreading the good news and making disciples, exercising our spiritual gifts in the sphere of influence God has given us. Spiritual lukewarmness, complacency and laziness are the sure road to ruin.

We ought to take counsel from what happened to the people of Laish. This is how the biblical writer described that place:

Then the five men departed and came to Laish and saw the people who were there, how they lived in security, after the manner of the Sidonians, quiet and unsuspecting, lacking nothing that is in the earth and possessing wealth, and how they were far from the Sidonians and had no dealings with anyone.

JUDGES 18:7

The Bible tells us their fate:

But the people of Dan took what Micah had made, and the priest who belonged to him, and they came to Laish, to a people quiet and unsuspecting, and struck them with the edge of the sword and burned the city with fire.

JUDGES 18:27

There was no one to save the people of Laish because they were affluent, alone, aloof, complacent, friendless and fatally vulnerable. Chilling. There is a strong warning here for all of us.

Scripture says, *"Therefore let anyone who thinks that he stands take heed lest he fall"* (1 Corinthians 10:12). The worst place to be spiritually is the place of perceived invincibility.

Are you actively and intentionally seeking to grow in holiness and godliness within a robust community of faith? Those who are doing so will survive and even thrive when things get tough. Those who don't, won't.

Complacency is deadly but contentment is godly. They are very different things, as you are about to see.

Learning Contentment

>> It may surprise you to know that another way to prepare for whatever lies ahead is learning contentment. In your group, have some members read the following Scriptures out loud and then discuss together the questions that follow:

I rejoiced in the Lord greatly that now at length you have revived your concern for me. You were indeed concerned for me, but you had no opportunity. Not that I am speaking of being in need, for I have learned in whatever situation I am to be content. I know how to be brought low, and I know how to abound. In any and every circumstance, I have learned the secret of facing plenty and hunger, abundance and need. I can do all things through him who strengthens me.

PHILIPPIANS 4:10-13

But godliness with contentment is great gain, for we brought nothing into the world, and we cannot take anything out of the world. But if we have food and clothing, with these we will be content. But those who desire to be rich fall into temptation, into a snare, into many senseless and harmful desires that plunge people into ruin and destruction.

1 TIMOTHY 6:6-9

Keep your life free from the love of money, and be content with what you have, for he has said, 'I will never leave you nor forsake you.' So we can confidently say, 'The Lord is my helper; I will not fear; what can man do to me?'

HEBREWS 13:5-6

>> In your group, talk about what you think "contentment" is. How is it contrasted with "complacency"? Come up with a consensus definition and write what you come up with in the spaces below. In addition, discuss these questions: According to these Scriptures, does contentment happen naturally to us? Why or why not? What was Paul's "secret"? How can "godliness with contentment" be a means of "great gain"? What happens to people who want to be wealthy? What are the things Paul told Timothy are our two basic necessities? How is it possible to be content with only those two things? In what ways are an awareness and appreciation for God's never-failing presence better than accumulating more wealth?

In a culture where aggressiveness, drivenness, ambition, outrage, competition, retaliation, greed, popularity, glowing fame and growing fortune are expected and rewarded if not idolized, an invitation to pursue contentment would likely be mocked and ridiculed. It sounds so old-fashioned and boring. Somewhere along the line the virtues of patience, calmness, civility, peacefulness and contentment have gone out of style. Too bad.

Are we in a better place because we have made this cultural shift?

The United States holds over 45% of the global pharmaceutical market, with $482 billion spent in 2018.[24]

At certain hours of the day you cannot escape the constant barrage of TV ads hawking drugs for everything from sleeplessness to depression to erectile dysfunction. Our society has become convinced that if there isn't a pill to cure every one of our ills, there ought to be. We have become a weak, agitated, entitled people, quick to condemn with a hair trigger set on outrage. Contentment is the farthest thing from most people's experience.

Stress, frustration, increased rage, disorganization, depression, out-of-control spending, burgeoning debt, restlessness, media and social media addictions, fatigue, anxiety, insecurity, exhaustion, and relational problems are fallout from our ravenous, consumer culture.

> We are on overload. The remedy is holiness and godliness and a return to biblical contentment.

What if suddenly as a nation we were confronted with deprivation that distilled life down to the basics, with barely enough food and clothing to survive? Those suffering natural disasters like severe storms, drought, outbreaks of disease, wildfires, etc. and manmade disasters such as acts of terror and war know what that is like. Those kinds of suffering expose character and shine the spotlight on where our faith and hope truly rest.

Is God enough? We will not know that God is all we need until He is all we have. Isn't it better to begin learning now that He will never fail us, rather than to desperately grope around in the dark when God pulls the plug and the lights go out on life as we now know it? This is not a trivial matter.

>> In this final exercise, I want to help you begin to put a lid on discontent and its partner-in-crime: the compulsion to find counterfeit joy through spending and accumulating stuff. The more we have and the more we think we need, the greater the shock will be when we lose it.

In advance of your group meeting, complete the following statements, asking God, as you work, for His wisdom:

When I am stressed, bored or unhappy I tend to spend money on ________

____

Though I/we don't really need it, I am leaning toward getting ________

____

It is just fun to go online and go on shopping sites and look at ________

____

>> Like you did earlier in this study, check one or two of the statements above. Choose something that indicates an area in which you are seriously struggling with being content with what you have and in which you are being tempted to buy something you really don't need.

Take some time in your group meeting to talk about your struggles with contentment and pray for one another that you would demonstrate the fruit of the Spirit of self-control.

Finally, as this book study is concluding, I encourage each person in the group to commit to staying in relationship with at least one other group member. Before you dismiss your final meeting, make sure you have a brother or sister with whom you will stay in contact. If you haven't already done so, add their contact information to your cell phone. Give each other a call within the next week to talk about how you are doing in following through on the points of application and obedience from this eighth study. Also take time to pray for each other over the phone, or better yet, in person.

It would be great if you develop a friendship, considering how to stir each other up to love and good deeds (Hebrews 10:24). Scripture says that two are better than one and three is even better (Ecclesiastes 4:9-12).

It's true confession time. Here is one recent battle with contentment that I have had. One of the TV channels I had to cut way back watching was HGTV. Though the Lord has given our family a wonderful home in western North Carolina that more than meets our needs, I started visually drooling over all the great renovations showcased on that channel. The result in my heart was an increasing amount of discontentment with our (totally paid off!) home and its furnishings. I even started looking around at rustic mountain cabins in our area, justifying all kinds of business plans and other reasons to move. Daily "new home for sale" ads popped up on my cell phone and so I had to stop looking at them, too. It was getting bad.

Once I realized I was being deceived, I shut off the flow of temptations and shut down that arena of discontent. I realized I didn't need these things to make me happy. Who I needed was God and He has more than met my needs. At that time, the Lord's peace returned and so did contentment.

In comparison to most of the world, our family is rich. In all likelihood, so is yours. Listen to these powerful words from Paul to his spiritual son, Timothy:

As for the rich in this present age, charge them not to be haughty, nor to set their hopes on the uncertainty of riches, but on God, who richly provides us with everything to enjoy. They are to do good, to be rich in good works, to be generous and ready to share, thus storing up treasure for themselves as a good foundation for the future, so that they may take hold of that which is truly life.

1 TIMOTHY 6:17-19

Take hold of that which is truly life. That's a good word. Jesus is the One who is truly life (John 14:6).

I encourage you to periodically go through your home and get rid of the clutter. Cheerfully give away stuff you don't use and don't need. Be ready and eager to share with those who have real needs. Have a blast doing it, knowing that you are helping people now and laying up treasure in heaven for the future (Matthew 6:19-21). You will never regret it.

There may come a time when sharing with one another generously will be the only way for God's people to survive. Why not develop this holy, godly habit now? Most people find they can live in much more freedom with less.

Take hold of Jesus. Never let Him go. Hold loosely to the rest. As God's Word says:

Therefore, since we are surrounded by so great a cloud of witnesses, let us also lay aside every weight, and sin which clings so closely, and let us run with endurance the race that is set before us, looking to Jesus, the founder and perfecter of our faith...

HEBREWS 12:1-2

We can't run far and we certainly will never finish the race set before us if we have vines tangled around our legs and a heavy load of bricks on our back. Whenever we are free from these things, we can fix our eyes on Jesus, Who is our Finish Line.

It's time to land this plane and taxi to the gate. The Conclusion will be my final words before you deplane and head home. For now, take to heart these words from the Bible:

For whatever was written in former days was written for our instruction, that through endurance and the encouragement of the Scriptures we might have hope. May the God of endurance and encouragement grant you to live in such harmony with one another, in accord with Christ Jesus, that together you may with one voice glorify the God and Father of our Lord Jesus Christ. Therefore welcome one another as Christ has welcomed you, for the glory of God...May the God of hope fill you with all joy and peace in believing, so that by the power of the Holy Spirit you may abound in hope.

ROMANS 15:4-7,13

unearthed

conclusion

At this stage in a book such as this, many people would hope for the latest prophetic revelation concerning the Second Coming of our Lord Jesus. I wish I had the inside scoop on God's timetable. Who wouldn't? However, if we have learned anything over the years, it should be that trying to predict the date or even the decade of Jesus' return is a sure path to failure.

Since the release of Hal Lindsey's and C.C. Carlson's mega-best seller (1970), *The Late, Great Planet Earth*, the evangelical world (and a chunk of the rest of humanity) has been on kind of rapture "high alert." Sort of a spiritual DEFCON 1 warning level concerning the return of Jesus.

In his books, Hal postulated that the Lord could very well come back by 1988 (his estimated timetable based on an interpretation of Matthew 24:34). He also suggested that the 1980's could very well see the end of history on planet Earth as we know it.[25]

No disrespect meant to our brother, since many people came to Jesus through Hal's books, but over 30 years have passed since the end of the 1980's and well, here we are.

One of the more famous (infamous?) claims to knowing the time when the culmination of the ages would come, was from the Jehovah's Witnesses. They boldly prophesied that the end of all kingdoms of the world and the full establishment of the kingdom of God would happen before the end of 1914.[26]

When Jesus unremarkably failed to honor their prediction, founder Charles Taze Russell could not bring himself to admit he had erred. The organization simply went into damage control, with Russell first proclaiming that what he predicted had indeed taken place,[27] though invisibly,[28] and then scolding their people for putting too much faith in fallible men.[29] Good grief.

Jesus said a lot of things to alert us to the days prior to His return, but one of the things He made clear is that it won't be according to our schedule:

Therefore keep watch, because you do not know on what day your Lord will come. But understand this: If the owner of the house had known at what time of night the thief was coming, he would have kept watch and would not have let his house be broken into. So you also must be ready, because the Son of Man will come at an hour when you do not expect him.

MATTHEW 24:42-44 NIV

Pretty cryptic, wouldn't you say? Purposefully so, I believe. Can you imagine how crazy things would get if we knew the exact date of Christ's return? People would go nuts buying stuff like Ferrari's on credit, knowing they would never have to make any payments! It's a good thing we do not know.

The key principle here (and in other places such as the parable of the ten virgins in Matthew 25:1-13) is to be watching and be ready. He may come today. It may be years or decades (or longer!) until He comes. We need to be ready either way.

Now I know that leaving room for the possibility that Christ's return may not be as imminent as many people think is no way to sell books. I mean, who wants to hear that? I really hope He comes back in my lifetime, but under normal biological circumstances that means three more decades, at the most. Statistically, at my age, I'm probably on the 13th or 14th hole of the golf course of life, but I might be on the 18th green and not know it. None of us knows how long we have left here on the earth and, I'm afraid, none of us knows when Jesus is coming back.

To be frank, I'm convinced it can be a profound waste of time to analyze every little nuance of the news in order to hopefully spot a heretofore hidden clue about the timetable of Christ's return. There are a lot better ways to occupy our time and I'll touch on those in a minute.

Having said that, I could never fault a believer living around 1943 for having been convinced that Adolph Hitler was the Antichrist. If ever anyone checked all the boxes to qualify as the Antichrist, he did. And he certainly was an antichrist (there is not just one). John wrote:

Dear children, the last hour is here. You have heard that the Antichrist is coming, and already many such antichrists have appeared. From this we know that the last hour has come.

1 JOHN 2:18 NLT

Did you catch that? John wrote in the late First Century. According to him, the "last hour" had already come by that time. That means we have been in the "last hour" for nearly 2000 years. And at the time of John's writing, many antichrists had already appeared on the scene.

Remember that to God a day is like a thousand years and a thousand years like a day (2 Peter 3:8).

To Christians in the 21st Century, it seems like Jesus ought to be here soon. After all, it's been over 2000 years, for heaven's sake. And there are certainly factors in history and in the world that indicate that His return could be close. But what if God decides to wait another "day"? Would that throw us for a loop? It shouldn't.

Having said that, I want to share one more personal encounter with the Lord that is helpful here, I believe. Then I'll wrap this up with some final words of exhortation.

A number of years ago I was going through a protracted time of praying for revival in America. I remember asking the Lord if we can expect an outpouring of His Spirit in these "last days." This is what I sensed Him saying:

"Yes, but it will only come through suffering."

Not exactly what I was hoping to hear. I'd much rather revival happened with great congregations of Christ followers gathered together worshipping the Lord and hearing His Word preached. And then, BOOM! the Holy Spirit falls and we are all changed. Now, I know that has occurred and can occur again. God can do whatever He wants.

But my sense is that in order for an affluent nation such as ours to bow its knee to its Creator, something(s) pretty drastic are going to have to happen to drive us to desperation. Right now, we are not desperate. Before we will see "God bless America" with revival, we will need to see "God break America" from its pride and false gods.

Thinking back to my lifeguard training, we were taught that if you see a potential drowning victim frantically splashing around with their head above water, they are not ready to be rescued. Our instructors told us to wait until their energy gets drained and they stop their frenzy, and then go and get them. That may sound a bit heartless and cruel, but it's not.

When a lifeguard seeks to make a rescue, if the lifeguard doesn't make it safely to shore or to the boat, there is no hope for the victim either. So, the lifeguard has the double duty of saving a life while not endangering his or her own. An individual flailing and frantically splashing can panic and jump on top of the lifeguard in their efforts to stay afloat. The lifeguard can drown. So you wait.

This analogy isn't perfect because there is no danger to God to come rescue us from our sinful ways. Jesus already risked it all for us. But there are some helpful parallels.

Right now, I'm not even sure our nation and its leaders are aware we are in water over our head. Nobody sees their need for a Savior until they realize they are "drowning." But with the current political climate becoming so polarized, so hostile, and so wearying, maybe more people will soon realize it is time to look elsewhere for help and hope.

With our affluence and self-sufficiency so deeply ingrained, it will likely take more than political division, however, to wake us up to our true condition.

> Suffering can accelerate the process of bringing us to desperation and to a place of such angst and helplessness and hopelessness that we finally look up again. God may indeed need to wait until we have exhausted all our own energetic efforts at self-salvation before He rescues.

What do I believe are our priorities now?

First, take to heart the amazing truth that how we live today can help determine when Jesus returns. In the 2 Peter passage we looked at earlier, there is a curious element the writer added to the mix:

Since all these things are thus to be dissolved, what sort of people ought you to be in lives of holiness and godliness, ***waiting for and hastening the coming of the day of God...***

2 PETER 3:11-12A (EMPHASIS MINE)

We may not be able to predict when Jesus is coming back, but we can somehow speed that day up as we live lives of holiness and godliness and eagerly wait (Philippians 3:20 NASB) for His return.

That's pretty amazing! Maybe you never thought that your life of righteous living, seeking first the kingdom of God, could pave the way for a speedier return of the Lord Jesus. I don't know about you, but that motivates me!

Second, be ready for spiritual battle by living according to who you are in Christ and putting on the armor of God. That includes the hope of our salvation. Paul wrote a great word to the Church in Thessalonica. It is worth quoting the full passage.

Now concerning the times and the seasons, brothers, you have no need to have anything written to you. For you yourselves are fully aware that the day of the Lord will come like a thief in the night. While people are saying, 'There is peace and security,' then sudden destruction will come upon them as labor pains come upon a pregnant woman, and they will not escape. But you are not in darkness, brothers, for that day to surprise you like a thief. For you are all children of light, children of the day. We are not of the night or of the darkness. So then let us not sleep, as others do, but let us keep awake and be sober. For those who sleep, sleep at night, and those who get drunk, are drunk at night. But since we belong to the day, let us be sober, having put on the breastplate of faith and love, and for a helmet the hope of salvation. For God has not destined us for wrath, but to obtain salvation through our Lord Jesus Christ, who died for us so that whether we are awake or asleep we might live for him. Therefore encourage one another and build one another up, just as you are doing.

1 THESSALONIANS 5:1-11

We are to be awake, sober and watchful, realizing that the days ahead will require the armor of God. Why? Because the battle will be rough. We need to "cast off the works of darkness and put on the armor of light" (Romans 13:12) because we are no longer darkness but are light in the Lord (Ephesians 5:8). That is who we are. We are children of the light.

Child of God, remember who you are.

Darkness can and, I believe, will be so strong in the days ahead that those who do not put on the helmet of the hope of salvation will lose the battles for their minds. The bottom line for the believer is that no matter how hard life becomes here on the earth *"God has not destined us for wrath, but to obtain salvation through our Lord Jesus Christ."* That is our hope. That will be the only hope that will sustain us.

"Don't forget the glory when the darkness comes."

Remember Peter's words that were quoted earlier in this book:

Therefore, preparing your minds for action, and being sober-minded, set your hope fully on the grace that will be brought to you at the revelation of Jesus Christ.
1 PETER 1:13

This is a Scripture that is life-giving to those currently afflicted for their faith in Christ. I believe there will be a day when they will be absolutely essential words to cling to here in the West.

Third, be about the task of fulfilling the Great Commission. Jesus gave us a surefire metric to gauge how close His return is:

And this gospel of the kingdom will be proclaimed throughout the whole world as a testimony to all nations, and then the end will come.
MATTHEW 24:14

A nation refers to an ethnic, culturally uniform people (Greek: ethnos), not a geographical region colored blue, pink, green or yellow on a map. For example, there are hundreds of "nations" inside the borders of the country of India. These nations are often referred to as "people groups." Most nations or people groups that have yet to be reached with the gospel live between 10° N. Latitude to 40° N. Latitude (AKA the 10/40 window). From the Global Frontier Missions website here is an update on our progress in reaching all nations with the gospel:

"It is estimated that of the 7.47 billion people alive in the world today, 3.15 billion of them live in unreached people groups with little or no access to the Gospel of Jesus Christ. According to the Joshua Project, there are approximately 17,098 unique people groups in the world with about 7153 of them considered unreached. The vast majority (95%) of these least reached groups exist in the 10/40 window and less than 3% of cross-cultural missionary work is done among these people."[30]

As you can see, we still have a long way to go to fulfill the "Great Commission" (see Matthew 28:18-20) where Christ mandated that we make disciples of all nations (ethni or people groups).

What can you do?

- Beseech the Lord of the harvest to send out His laborers to the harvest fields of reaching the unreached peoples (Matthew 9:37,38); there are ministries that will provide specific guidelines in how to pray for unreached nations
- Give generously to missionaries and ministries that are reputable (look for the ECFA seal on their websites) and which are specifically targeting the unreached
- Update your passport and ask God to send you (short-term or long-term) to help reach the unreached; every mission organization has opportunities to serve...not only on the field, but also in support and administrative roles domestically

Finally, ask God to make you His bold and fearless witness wherever you live. We are not called to be nice; we are called to be nuclear. We are not supposed to leave people alone; we are supposed to love them enough to bring the good news of God's grace and warn of the danger of rejecting it. We are not saved to fit in to the culture; we are saved to radically confront it in love and rescue those who are trapped in it (Jude 22). We can and must do this whether Jesus is coming back tomorrow or sometime in the more distant future.

I think it is kind of funny that right after Jesus ascended into heaven and the disciples were staring up into the sky, two angels basically had to tell them that He wasn't coming back for a while. A 2000-year-old stiff neck would not have been fun.

Before Jesus left, this brief conversation between our Lord and His disciples is a poignant reminder for us:

So when they had come together they asked him, 'Lord, will you at this time restore the kingdom to Israel?' He said to them, 'It is not for you to know times or seasons that the Father has fixed by his own authority. But you will receive power when the Holy Spirit has come upon you, and you will be my witnesses in Jerusalem and in all Judea and Samaria, and to the end of the earth.

ACTS 1:6-8

You and I have that same Holy Spirit with that same power for being Christ's witnesses that the disciples had, the power of Christ's resurrection.

Let's boldly go as Christ's ambassadors to share the good news...whether across the street or around the world. God will be with us no matter what happens. Our hope is in Him.

Let's make the apostle Paul's heartbeat ours as well:

...that I may know him and the power of his resurrection, and may share in his sufferings, becoming like him in his death, that by any means possible I may attain the resurrection from the dead. Not that I have already obtained this or am already perfect, but I press on to make it my own, because Christ Jesus has made me his own. Brothers, I do not consider that I have made it my own. But one thing I do: forgetting what lies behind and straining forward to what lies ahead, I press on toward the goal for the prize of the upward call of God in Christ Jesus.

PHILIPPIANS 3:10-16

Will you please join me in prayer one last time?

PRAY

Dear Father, knowing that You are watching over me and over everything that is going on around me gives me a deep, settled sense of peace. Nothing in the entire universe throughout all of history has ever escaped Your notice. Not one single thing. And nothing in all creation can ever separate me from the love You have for me in Christ. That love fills me with a joy like nothing else. Now that these studies are complete, I ask that You would set me on a strong, steady path of knowing the Lord Jesus and the great power of His resurrection. Yes, and even to share in His sufferings as You so will. Thank You that Jesus has made me His own. By Your grace, I will press on to follow Your call onward and upward in Christ. And when it's all over, I will find You to be the greatest prize of all. I can't wait to see You...soon, I hope. Amen.

End Notes

1. C.S. Lewis, *The Problem with Pain* (New York: Harper Collins, 1940, 1996).
2. Elisabeth Elliot, *Suffering is Never for Nothing* (Nashville, TN: B&H Publishing Group, 2019).
3. Carl Jung as quoted in Joe Bayly, *The View from a Hearse* (Bloomington, IN: Warhorn Media, 2014).
4. Barnabas Aid, September/October, 2019 issue.
5. Josef Tson (sometimes spelled Ton), *Suffering, Martyrdom and Rewards in Heaven* (New York: The Romanian Missionary Society, 1997).
6. Barnabas Aid, September/October, 2019 issue.
7. Ibid.
8. Ibid.
9. Ibid.
10. Ibid.
11. Barnabas Aid, *Prayer Guide* September/October, 2019.
12. Barnabas Aid, September/October, 2019 issue.
13. Dale Hurd, *'Jesus Loves You' Lands VA Real Estate Agent in Hot Water: 'Targeted Discrimination Against Christians'* (CBNNEWS.com, August 19, 2019).
14. Nik Ripken, *The Insanity of God* (Nashville, TN: B&H Publishing Group, 2013).
15. Richard Wurmbrand, *Tortured for Christ* (Bartlesville, OK: Living Sacrifice Book Company, 1967, 1998).
16. Ibid.
17. Ibid.
18. Ibid.
19. Ibid.

20. Ibid.
21. Alaine Pakkala interview with Rich Miller, August 16, 2019.
22. Ibid.
23. Tson, *Suffering, Martyrdom and Rewards in Heaven.*
24. https:/www.statista.com/study/10708/US-pharmaceutical-industry-statista-dossier/
25. Hal Lindsey, *The 1980's: Countdown to Armageddon* (New York: Bantam Books, 1982).
26. *Studies in the Scriptures – The Time Is at Hand* (1889) 1911 ed. P. 99.
27. *Yearbook* 1975 pp. 72,73
28. *Watchtower* 1993 Jan 15 p. 5
29. *Watchtower* 1914 Nov 1 pp. 325-326 reprints p. 5565
30. Global Frontier Missions website, October 17, 2019.

AUTHOR'S NOTE: Though not quoted in the pages of *unearthed*, Dr. Richard A. Swanson's book, *Contentment*, was a very helpful stimulus toward the writing of a portion of *Study Eight* as well as to my own life personally.

Isaiah 35

The wilderness and the dry land shall be glad; the desert shall rejoice and blossom like the crocus; it shall blossom abundantly and rejoice with joy and singing. The glory of Lebanon shall be given to it, the majesty of Carmel and Sharon. They shall see the glory of the Lord, the majesty of our God. Strengthen the weak hands, and make firm the feeble knees. Say to those who have an anxious heart, "Be strong; fear not! Behold, your God will come with vengeance, with the recompense of God. He will come and save you." Then the eyes of the blind shall be opened, and the ears of the deaf unstopped; then shall the lame man leap like a deer, and the tongue of the mute sing for joy. For waters break forth in the wilderness, and streams in the desert; the burning sand shall become a pool, and the thirsty ground springs of water; in the haunt of jackals, where they lie down, the grass shall become reeds and rushes. And a highway shall be there, and it shall be called the Way of Holiness; the unclean shall not pass over it. It shall belong to those who walk on the way; even if they are fools, they shall not go astray. No lion shall be there, nor shall any ravenous beast come up on it; they shall not be found there, but the redeemed shall walk there. And the ransomed of the Lord shall return and come to Zion with singing; everlasting joy shall be upon their heads; they shall obtain gladness and joy, and sorrow and sighing shall flee away.

NOTES

NOTES

Make sure to get all three studies in "the unusual series":

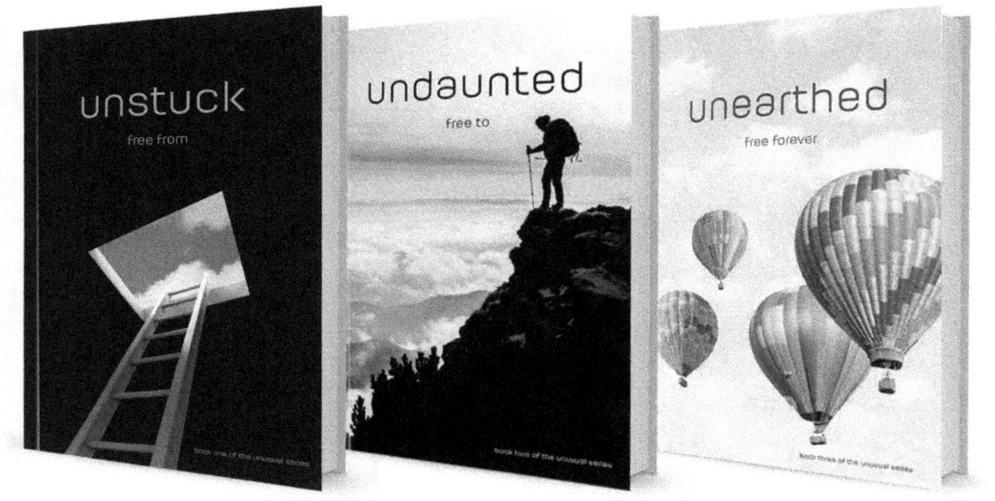

unstuck: free from

Most Christians are stuck and don't know how to get free. In these eight heart-transforming studies, you will tackle the big obstacles to growth in Christ and discover God's powerful liberating truths for your life.

undaunted: free to

Once we have experienced freedom in Christ, we can live life courageously in the power of the Spirit. Learn how freedom is the gateway to fruitful ministry in... prayer, worship, evangelism, humanitarian service, standing against injustice and more!

unearthed: free forever

Your future hope and freedom gives you strength to endure present trials. This book will help get you really ready for all the world may throw at you in the days to come. Find out how to be a catalyst to spreading that hope to others, no matter what lies ahead.

CPSIA information can be obtained
at www.ICGtesting.com
Printed in the USA
JSHW042125140320
4721JS00002B/6

9 780996 972536